The State Courts

Compiled By
Robert A. Carp, Ronald Stidham,
and Kenneth L. Manning

CQ Press Custom and Online Books

CQ Press Custom and Online Books

2300 N Street, NW, Suite 800
Washington, DC 20037
Phone: 202-729-1900; toll-free, 1-866-4CQ-PRESS (1-866-427-7737)

Web: www.cqpress.com

CONTENTS

Robert A. Carp, Ronald Stidham, and Kenneth L. Manning, *The State Courts,* (Washington, DC: CQ Press, 2010).

1. PREFACE

We have sought to prepare a readable, comprehensive book about state courts and their impact on our daily lives. It is designed primarily for students in courses in judicial process and behavior, constitutional law, law and society, American government and politics, and state government and politics.

The book is written with minimal resort to the jargon and theoretical vocabulary of political science and law. Although at times it is necessary and useful to employ some technical terms and evoke some theoretical concepts in our look at state courts, we address the basic questions on a level that is accessible to the educated layperson. For students who may desire more specialized explanations or who wish to explore more deeply some of the issues we touch on, the glossary, notes, and suggested resources contain ample resources for such quests. In addition, we have included further thought and discussion questions at the end of each chapter that provide an opportunity for more in-depth consideration of the general themes of the book.

We avoid stressing any particular theoretical framework for the study of state courts and legal questions, such as a judicial realist perspective or a systems model approach. Instructors partial to the tenets of modern behavioralism will find much here to gladden their hearts, but we also have included some of the insights that more traditional scholarship has provided over the years. The book reflects the contributions not only of political scientists and legal scholars but also of historians, psychologists, court administrators, and journalists.

Throughout the text we are mindful of the interrelation between the state courts and public policy. We work with the premise that significant portions of our lives—as individuals and as a state—are affected by what our judges choose to do and refrain from doing. We reject the often-held assumption that only liberals make public policy and conservatives practice restraint; rather, we believe that to some degree all judges engage in this normal and inevitable activity. In the chapters that follow we examine why this has come to be, how it works, and the consequences for America today.

Chapter 1 provides an introduction to the various types of laws that have developed in the United States. We also describe the basic functions of the state courts in the context of a system that includes the federal courts. These functions may be divided into three main areas: dispute resolution, application of the law, and legal interpretation. It is here that we first note that state judges, as they interpret laws, may also engage in policymaking to some extent.

Chapter 2 focuses on the judicial systems in the various states and includes two figures that contrast a simplified court structure (California) with a more complex one (New York). The chapter also covers courts of limited jurisdiction, the increasing use of administrative hearings (in place of litigation), and the expanding role of state supreme courts in important areas of policymaking, such as same-sex marriage. The statistical tables on state court workload reflect the most recent available data.

In Chapter 3 we outline the jurisdiction of state courts and discuss the political and nonjusticiable realms of American life into which judges in principle are not supposed to enter. We believe that a full understanding of how judges affect citizens' lives requires some knowledge of the substantive areas into which state jurists may not roam.

Chapter 4, on state judges, describes the various methods by which states choose those who will occupy the bench. In addition, it highlights the most recent research on diversity on the state courts, the increasing competition in state judicial races, and the mounting sums of money being spent on judicial elections.

Chapter 5 focuses on lawyers, litigants, and interest groups in the state courts. We discuss the lawyers who represent the state government in the handling of criminal cases, both in the trial courts and in the appellate courts. We also look at the private attorneys who are active in criminal and civil cases. Litigants, both those involved in private legal disputes and those involved in public law cases, are also dealt with in this chapter. A distinction is made between the goals of litigants and lawyers involved in these two broad categories of disputes. Finally, we examine the influence of interest groups in the states' judicial process. Interest groups have two basic methods by which they may affect the direction of state court decisions: involvement in test cases and the submission of *amicus curiae* briefs.

In Chapter 6 we turn our attention to how judges reach their decisions. We first outline those aspects of the decision-making process that are common to all judges, in the context of the legal subculture (the traditional legal reasoning model explaining judges' decisions) and the democratic subculture (a number of extralegal factors that appear to be associated with judges' policy decisions). We then examine the special case of decision making in collegial courts. We explore the assumptions of cue theory, small-group analysis, attitude theory, and the rational choice model.

Chapter 7 focuses on implementation and impact of judicial policies. First, we analyze why some judicial rulings are implemented completely and why others are implemented only partially or not at all. The roles of various persons involved in the implementation process are also examined. We conclude the chapter with a brief discussion of the strengths and weaknesses of the courts as policymakers in the American system of government.

ACKNOWLEDGMENTS

Charisse Kiino, Lorna Notsch, Nancy Loh, and the entire team at CQ Press encouraged and assisted us throughout the development of this book and to them we offer our sincere thanks. An expression of gratitude is also in order for Carolyn Goldinger, who did an excellent job of copyediting the final version of the text. We assume responsibility for any errors that remain.

To Albert Bradford, a highly respected and much-valued friend for many decades

R.A.C.

To the memory of my mother, Margaret Pauline Robinette Stidham

R.S.

To my daughter, Katherine, and son, Kenneth

K.L.M.

Robert A. Carp, Ronald Stidham, and Kenneth L. Manning, *The State Courts*, (Washington, DC: CQ Press, 2010).

1. AN INTRODUCTION TO LAW AND COURTS

It is something many of us have experienced. The flashing lights of a police car in your rear-view mirror. A uniformed officer approaching your vehicle, asking for a driver's license and auto registration. A lump in your throat and a sinking feeling that this is going to cost you. Chances are that if you have gotten a traffic ticket in the United States, you have had some experience, however minor, with a state court.

A motor vehicle citation is a formal accusation by a law enforcement officer that you broke a state law. To resolve this matter, you must answer to a state court. Many who receive a traffic citation concede that the charge is true—that they broke the law as accused in the ticket and, consequently, agree to pay the scheduled fine by remitting payment to the proper court. Sometimes, however, individuals appeal the ticket and seek a trial. Or they may seek a hearing before a judge to present mitigating evidence or to ask for leniency. Regardless of the outcome, the resolution of a traffic ticket is one of the most common ways that people interact with a court in the United States.

In ordinary circumstances, courts tend not to get much public attention. Indeed, courts are government institutions that usually work in the background of daily political life in states. The media take notice as legislatures make laws, wrangle with budgets, and negotiate compromises on the important issues of the day. Governors attract interest as they press forward with their own agendas, usually locked in a back-and-forth relationship with the legislature in their respective states while overseeing state bureaucracies that carry out the laws. State courts, on the other hand, tend to garner relatively little attention from the press and the public. When courts are on the front page of daily life, it is usually because of a particularly notable case: a controversial ruling that raises eyebrows, a high profile litigant, or an especially awful crime.

But even though they may not be in the forefront of public thought, courts matter a great deal in a functioning democracy. They resolve disputes that inevitably arise between people. They are one of the linchpins in the criminal justice system, a system that is crucial to public safety and order. They tackle some of the most profound legal and moral questions that arise in our society, answering tough questions about what the law means and how it is interpreted.

This book examines state courts in the United States. These judicial institutions carry the vast majority of the load of cases and legal disputes in the country. In many ways, the state courts are the backbone of the American legal system, the place where justice in the legal system is most commonly carried out, and the courts that are closest to the American people.

STATE COURTS IN A FEDERAL SYSTEM

As the Revolutionary War came to an end in 1781, the thirteen colonies officially ratified the first national constitution—the Articles of Confederation. This charter created a federal system, a political system with a national government over state, regional, or territorial governments. But, as events quickly revealed, the central government created by the articles was too weak to be effective. As a result, the states sent delegates to a convention in Philadelphia in 1787 to amend the articles. Instead, they drafted a new constitution. The nation's founders faced a dizzying array of issues to decide, and one of the most profound questions was the fundamental structure of government.

The U.S. Constitution drawn up in the summer of 1787 maintained a federal structure of government. A unitary system—a political system with only one government—was never under serious consideration. Such a system would have been extremely difficult to administer over a geographically sprawling nation that stretched from Massachusetts to Georgia. In addition, a unitary system would have created a centralized government with power in the hands of a few. Following their experiences with the British monarchy, the founders were deeply skeptical of concentrated political power and the opportunity for abuse it presented.

But in creating a federal system, the founders were presented with a difficult dilemma. How much uniformity should the federal government require of the states and how much authority should the states have to handle their own affairs? Too much federal oversight of state matters presented problems, but so did too little oversight, including the potential for interstate conflict.

Ultimately, the U.S. Constitution recognizes that states have their own constitutions, government structures, and legal systems. Although the Constitution mandates that all state governments have some form of representative democracy, the states are given significant latitude to create their own government institutions and procedures. At the same time, the U.S. Constitution stipulates that when a conflict arises between a state law and federal law, federal law reigns supreme. Moreover, numerous constitutional amendments, judicial rulings, and laws passed by Congress have imposed some level of uniform action or requirements upon the states. At the same time, many of these same federal stipulations allow significant state-to-state variation. A study of state courts therefore is an exercise in comparisons and contrasts. Such a study will inevitably find common characteristics and themes in these courts, while also recognizing the structural, procedural, and political diversity that exists among these important organizations.

THE ROLE OF COURTS

As institutions that are part of a structure of governance, courts perform a variety of important functions. Yet many people are unaware or unclear about all that courts do. We know that courts handle criminal cases and traffic tickets. We know that courts are the venues where law suits are filed and litigated. But beyond these tasks, what are the primary responsibilities of state courts? We point to three: dispute resolution, application of the law, and legal interpretation. These three functions are not exhaustive in describing the work that courts do, nor are they mutually exclusive. For example, courts usually resolve disputes by applying the law. And keep in mind, too, that in each of these roles the court may make public policy and in that way engage in behavior that is similar to lawmaking by state legislatures. Still, these three responsibilities go a long way in describing the basic functions of courts in the states.

Dispute Resolution

One of the most common chores that state courts perform is resolving disputes between disagreeing parties. How disputes are resolved between quarreling individuals, corporations, or government entities reveals much about the level and quality of the rule of law in a society. Without an orderly, peaceful process for dispute resolution, either chaos prevails or the largest gang of thugs or those with the strongest fists controls society.

Basically, all cases that land before a court involve a dispute that the parties want resolved. These disagreements can range from the very small to very large, from the deeply personal to the purely economic. A customer unhappy that her dry cleaner has ruined a favorite dress, a divorcing couple sparring over shared property, insurance companies clashing over a payout in an auto accident, two corporations engaged in a multimillion dollar lawsuit over a big business deal gone sour—all of these present opportunities for courts to resolve a dispute. Naturally, courts are not the only venue or means to resolve disputes. The parties may try to negotiate a mutually agreeable settlement on their own; they may employ a mediator or arbitrator to reach agreement; or they may even resort to violence or other extralegal actions. Resolving disputes in court, however, offers the advantage of having the state preside over the process with the ability of the government to enforce agreements and any decision by the judge. In addition, the resolution is achieved in a peaceful way that avoids violence.

Application of the Law

Courts are also called upon to apply the law, that is, to enact consequences as provided for by law when a court is presented with evidence that is determined to be factual. This function is what primarily occurs in criminal matters, when courts are asked to rule on the validity of criminal charges. If a court reviews evidence and finds the charges to be valid beyond a reasonable doubt, the judge or jury orders applicable legal consequences—a fine, imprisonment, even death in some circumstances.

Consider the following example. Police arrest a suspect, and he is presented to a judge to be charged formally with committing a crime. The judge may be asked to grant bail for the suspect, based upon certain information presented to the judge. Depending on the various circumstances involved, the law may or may not allow bail. If bail is allowed, the law may provide guidelines for the appropriate amount. It is then up to the judge to weigh the evidence presented to her and to decide what amount of bail, if any, is appropriate and consistent with the law. The judge may not deviate from the law; she must apply it to the facts and evidence presented to her. Much of the workload of state courts involves criminal matters—entailing everything from routine hearings to full criminal trials. Consequently, a lot of what state courts do involves applying the law to specific fact patterns and circumstances.

Legal Interpretation

Words can sometimes mean different things to different people. This is certainly true when it comes to specific provisions of state constitutions or the laws passed by state legislatures. In fact, laws are filled with words that are inherently vague, using terms such as *excessive, reasonable,* and *due process.* Many legal terms are therefore subject to different interpretations. In other instances, the text of the law may be specific in nature, but behind those words may lie important principles and ideas that are less precise and require interpretation. For example, the Massachusetts Constitution was written in 1780 and, like the U.S. Constitution, it protects an individual's "freedom of speech." Does it protect the right to send a text message on your mobile phone? Put a bumper sticker on your car? The Constitution says "speech," but what exactly is "speech?" This simple six letter word can mean many different things, and it is ripe for interpretation and explanation. Legal interpretation may also occur as the result of simple inconsistency in the law. Given the sheer volume of laws passed over many decades, it is inevitable that the language of one law may conflict with another. At the end of the day, it is the courts that step in to clear up these differences, to interpret what the law means.

Most legal interpretation at the state level is done by state supreme courts. As the final arbiters of state law, these courts of last resort render decisions about what the law means and to clear up any conflicts or inconsistencies. That is not to say, however, that lower state courts are prohibited from engaging in legal interpretation. But such instances are quite rare overall, and the vast majority of the work of lower state courts involves law application and dispute resolution.

SOURCES OF LAW IN THE UNITED STATES

We recognize that state courts are vitally important to resolving disputes that arise under the law, applying the law to specific fact patterns, and interpreting the meaning of the law. But what is **law?** And where does it come from?

A useful definition of American law postulates that "law is a social norm the infraction of which is sanctioned in threat or in fact by the application of physical force by a party possessing the socially recognized privilege of so acting."[1] This definition suggests that law comprises three basic elements—force, official authority, and regularity—the combination of which differentiates law from mere custom or morals in society.

In an ideal society, force would never have to be exercised. In our imperfect world, the threat of its use is a foundation of any law-abiding society. Although the government may use substitutes for physical force, such as confiscation of property or imposition of fines, the possibility of physical punishment must nevertheless remain to deter a potential lawbreaker. The right to apply this force constitutes the official element of the definition of law. The party that exercises this right of physical coercion represents a valid legal authority. Finally, the term *regularity,* as used in the legal sense, can be likened to its use by scientists. Although the term does not reflect absolute certainty, it does suggest uniformity and consistency. The law calls for a degree of predictability, of regularity, in the way individuals are expected to behave or to be treated by the state. In American society, this emphasis on regularity is manifested by adherence to prior court decisions and precedents (the **common law** doctrine of **stare decisis**) and by the mandate of the Fourteenth Amendment to the U.S. Constitution, which forbids the state to "deny to any person within its **jurisdiction** the *equal protection* of the law" (emphasis added).[2]

Where does U.S. law come from? At first the question seems a bit simpleminded. A typical response might be, "Law comes from legislatures; that is what Congress and the state legislatures do." This answer is not wrong, but it is far from adequate. Law comes from a large variety of sources. Moreover, it comes primarily from two different levels of government: federal and state.

Constitutions

The U.S. Constitution is the primary source of law in the United States, as it claims to be in Article VI: "This Constitution ... shall be the supreme Law of the Land; and the Judges in every State shall be bound thereby, any Thing in the Constitution or Laws of any State to the Contrary notwithstanding." Therefore, none of the other types of law may stand if they are in conflict with the Constitution. But each state also has its own constitution. Although the U.S. Constitution stipulates that all local laws must yield to national supremacy, states have significant constitutional lawmaking authority.

Acts of Legislative Bodies

Laws passed by state legislatures constitute a sizable bulk of law in the United States. Statutes requiring the payment of taxes to state government and state laws forbidding theft or assault are examples. But many other types of legislative bodies also enact statutes and ordinances that regulate our lives. County commissioners (also known as county judges or boards of selectmen), for example, may act as legislative bodies for the various counties within the states.

Likewise, city councils serve in a legislative capacity when they pass ordinances, set property-tax rates, establish building codes, and so on at the municipal level. In addition are the almost 50,000 "special districts" throughout the country, each of which is headed by an elected or appointed body that acts in a legislative capacity. Some examples are school districts, fire prevention districts, water districts, and municipal utility districts.

Decisions of Quasi-Legislative and Quasi-Judicial Bodies

Sprinkled vertically and horizontally throughout the U.S. governmental structure are thousands of boards, agencies, commissions, departments, and so on, whose primary function is not to legislate or to adjudicate, but which still may be called on to make rules or to render decisions that are semi-legislative or semi-judicial in character. The job of the Illinois Pollution Control Board is to protect the environment of the state of Illinois. When the board hands down rules on industrial plant emissions, waste disposal regulations, and other similar policy, it is acting in a semi-or quasi-judicial capacity.

The U.S. Securities and Exchange Commission (SEC) is not a lawmaking body either, but when it determines that a particular company has run afoul of the securities laws or rules on a firm's qualification to be listed on the New York Stock Exchange, it becomes a source of law in the United States. In effect, the SEC makes rules and decisions that affect a person's or a company's behavior and for which penalties are imposed for noncompliance. Although decisions of such agencies may be appealed to or reviewed by the courts, they are binding unless they are overturned by a judicial entity.

A university's board of regents may also be a source of law for the students, faculty, and staff members covered by its jurisdiction. These boards may set rules on matters such as which persons may lawfully enter the campus, procedures to be followed before a staff member may be fired, or definitions of plagiarism. Violations of these rules or procedures carry penalties backed by the full force of the law.

Orders and Rulings of Political Executives

Civics classes teach that legislatures make the law and executives enforce the law. That is essentially true, but political executives also have some lawmaking capacity. This lawmaking occurs when presidents, governors, mayors, or others fill in the details of statutes passed by legislative bodies, and sometimes when they promulgate orders purely in their executive capacity.

When Congress passes reciprocal trade agreement legislation, the goal is to encourage other countries to lower trade and tariff barriers to U.S.-produced goods, in exchange for which the United States will do the same. But there are so many thousands of goods, almost 200 countries, and countless degrees of setting up or lowering trade barriers. What to do? The customary practice is for Congress to set basic guidelines for the reciprocal lowering of trade barriers and allow the president, or people acting for the president, to decide how much to regulate a given tariff on any given commodity for a particular country. These executive orders of the president are published in the *Federal Register* and carry the full force of law. In fact, at the national level more than 70,000 pages of new rules are churned out each year.[3]

Another example of an executive order came in November 2001, when Americans were still in shock from the 9/11 terrorist attacks. President George W. Bush signed an order that allowed prosecutors to bypass the U.S. criminal justice system and swiftly convict foreigners involved in acts of terror. Under the Bush order, the chief executive determined who should be tried in the American court system and who should be prosecuted in a military court set up by the secretary of defense in whatever country he deemed appropriate.[4] Barack Obama campaigned fiercely against these military tribunals, and indeed he suspended them by executive order within hours of taking office in January 2009. Four months after taking office, however, Obama issued executive orders that re-started the tribunals (with a few new legal protections) for a small number of detainees.[5] "This is the best way to protect our country, while upholding our deeply held values," he said.[6]

Likewise, at the state level, when a legislature delegates to the governor the right to "fill in the details of legislation," the state executive uses his **ordinance-making power,** which also is a type of lawmaking capacity. Political executives may promulgate orders that within certain narrow but important realms, constitute the law of the land. After a natural disaster such as a flood or tornado, a mayor may declare an official state of emergency that empowers her to issue binding rules of behavior for a limited period of time. A curfew ordering persons to be off the streets at a given hour is an example of a law made by a municipal chief executive; such a state of affairs existed in Galveston, Texas, after Hurricane Ike in 2008. Although limited and usually temporary, such orders are law, and violations invoke penalties.

Judicial Decisions

Civics classes also teach that judges interpret the law. So they do, but judges also make law as they interpret it. And judicial decisions themselves constitute a body of law in the United States. All the thousands of court decisions that have been handed down by federal and state judges over the past two centuries are part of the **corpus juris**—the body of law—of the United States.

Judicial decisions may be grounded in or surround a variety of entities: any of the above-mentioned sources of law, past decisions of other judges, or legal principles that have evolved over the centuries. Judicial decisions may also be grounded in the common law, that is, those written (and sometimes unwritten) legal traditions and principles that have served as the basis of court decisions and accepted human behavior for many centuries. One example is common law marriage. If a couple lives together as husband and wife for a specified period of years, the common law may be invoked to have their relationship recognized as a legal marriage.

TYPES OF LAW

Now that we have examined the wellsprings of American law, we take a brief look at the vessels that contain the laws; that is, we define or explain the formal types of categories of law. Remember that types of law are not necessarily mutually exclusive.

Codified (or Code) Law

Unlike the United States, most countries (including most of Europe and Latin America) refer to themselves as code law countries. A code is a body of laws that has been enacted by a national legislature. These laws address virtually all aspects of the body politic, are often detailed, and are arranged in an orderly, systematic, and comprehensive manner. The U.S. legal system is often seen from abroad as a hodgepodge of legislative acts, judicial decisions, unwritten legal traditions, and so on.

Statutory Law and Common Law

Statutory law is the type of law enacted by a legislative body such as Congress, a state legislature, or a city council, although it could also include the written orders of various quasi-legislative bodies. The key is that the enactments be in written form and be addressed to the needs of society as a whole. Examples of statutory law would be a congressional act increasing Social Security payments or a statute passed by a state legislature authorizing the death penalty for first-degree murder. Statutory law is often contrasted with the common law, which is a less-orderly compilation of traditions, principles, and legal practices that have been handed down from one generation of lawyers and judges to the next. Because much of the common law is not systematically codified and delineated, as is statutory law, it is sometimes referred to as the unwritten law. That description is not entirely accurate. Much of the common law exists in the form of court decisions and legal precedents that are in written form. The common law is known for its flexibility and capacity to change as it evolves in response to the changing needs and values of society.

Civil Law and Criminal Law

Civil law deals with disagreements between individuals, such as a dispute over ownership of private property. Civil law also deals with corporations, admiralty matters, and contracts. **Criminal law** pertains to offenses against the state itself—actions that may be directed against a person but that are deemed to be offensive to society as a whole. **Crimes** such as driving while intoxicated, armed robbery, and so on are punishable by fines or imprisonment.

Equity

Equity is best understood when contrasted with law; the primary difference between the two terms lies in the remedy involved. In law, the only remedy is financial compensation; in equity, a judge is free to issue a remedy that will either prevent or cure the wrong that is about to happen. Because in many circumstances monetary settlements are inappropriate or inadequate, equity allows judges a degree of flexibility that they would not otherwise have. Suppose you are the owner of an old cabin located in the center of town and that this structure was the first built in the community. You wish to preserve it because of its historic value, but the city decides to expand the adjacent street and thereby destroy the cabin. Your remedy at law is to ask the city for monetary compensation, but to you this is inadequate. The cabin has little intrinsic value, but as a historic object it is priceless. You may wish to ask a judge to issue a writ in equity that might order the city to move the cabin to another site or order the city to reconsider its plan to widen the street.

Private Law

Private law deals with the rights and obligations that private individuals and institutions have when they relate to one another. Much civil law is in this category, because it covers subjects such as contracts between private persons and corporations and statutes pertaining to marriage and divorce.

Public Law

Public law addresses the relationship that individuals and institutions have with the state as a sovereign entity. The government makes laws in its capacity as the primary political unit to which all owe allegiance; in turn, the government is obliged to preserve and protect the citizens who live within its jurisdiction. Public law also deals with obligations that citizens have to the government, such as paying taxes or serving in the armed forces, or it may pertain to services or obligations that the state owes to its citizenry, such as laws providing for unemployment compensation or statutes protecting property rights. Criminal law also falls into this broad category, as do laws that deal with diverse subjects such as defense, welfare, and taxation. Two subheadings in this category are administrative law and constitutional law.

Administrative Law. The decisions and regulations set forth by the various administrative agencies of the government are the substance of administrative law. Agencies, such as state environmental offices or a city health department, are empowered to oversee implementation or carry out specific mandates established by a legislative body. When one of these agencies promulgates rules or guidelines about how it intends to carry out its regulatory functions, the rules become part of administrative law.

Constitutional Law. Basically, constitutional law is the compilation of all court rulings on the meaning of the various words, phrases, and clauses in the U.S. Constitution. Although all courts have the authority to perform this function, the U.S. Supreme Court has the final say about questions of constitutional law. In 1952, during the Korean War, the United States was faced with a strike by the unions against the nation's steel producers. Because President Harry S. Truman believed that a steel strike would impair the production of armaments needed for the war, he decided to seize and run the steel mills in the name of the United States. Truman claimed that he had "inherent powers" under Article II of the Constitution to do this, citing his power as "Commander in Chief of the Army and Navy" and that "the executive power shall be vested in [the] president." The Supreme Court disagreed with Truman and ruled that the chief executive did not have inherent authority to seize and operate the steel mills—even in time of emergency—without specific congressional authorization.[7]

State Law and Federal Law

Laws passed by one of the fifty state legislatures, ordinances promulgated by a state governor, and decisions handed down by a state court all constitute the corpus juris of a single state. They are compelling only for the citizens of that state and for outsiders who reside or do business there. State laws must not conflict with either federal law or anything in the U.S. Constitution. Examples of state law are Wisconsin's income tax for those who reside within its boundaries and New Mexico's criminal penalty for bank robbery. Federal law is made up of acts of Congress, presidential orders, U.S. court decisions, and so on. This body of law applies throughout the United States and usually pertains to topics that are relevant to persons in more than just one state. Examples include a congressional act forbidding the transportation of a stolen car across state lines and a U.S. Supreme Court decision outlawing prayer in the public schools. As with state law, federal law must be in harmony with the strictures of the U.S. Constitution.

SUMMARY

In this chapter we looked briefly at the role of courts in the U.S. federal system. We reviewed three primary jobs that courts do in the United States. We also discussed the law—its sources, its basic types, and its functions in society. Finally, we noted that Americans' contentiousness as a people has been channeled largely through the legal and court systems. As a consequence, the high priests of the judicial temples, the judges, have a considerable effect on Americans' personal lives and on their evolution as a society and political entity.

FURTHER THOUGHT AND DISCUSSION QUESTIONS

1. In the United States today almost 7.2 million people, about one of every forty-five, are either incarcerated or on probation or parole. Is this a sign of the inherent lawlessness of the American people, or is it evidence that the United States is a nation that believes in strict law enforcement?

2. Americans are known internationally for their high rate of filing lawsuits, but many other nations, particularly developing countries, are beginning to close the gap. Is this a sign of progress or regression on their part?

3. How many U.S. citizens would be willing to break the law and risk imprisonment if their economic survival depended on it? If they believed the law was illegal and unjustified? If they felt the law violated a higher moral or religious belief? If they felt the law unfairly violated their individual liberties?

Notes

1. Stephen D. Ford, *The American Legal System: Its Dynamics and Limits* (St. Paul, Minn.: West, 1974), 13. Our elaborations on this definition of law are borrowed from chapter 1 of Ford's text.
2. U.S. Constitution, Amendment XIV, section 1.
3. Dahlia Lithwick, "Imagining Life Without Lawyers," *Newsweek*, February 9, 2009, 20.
4. Patty Reinert, "Bush Defends Military Tribunals," *Houston Chronicle*, November 27, 2001.
5. Lara Jakes, "Obama Revives Terror Tribunals," *Houston Chronicle*, May 15, 2009, A11.
6. William Glaberson, "Obama to Keep Tribunals; Stance Angers Some Backers," *New York Times*, May 16, 2009.
7. *Youngstown Sheet & Tube Co. v. Sawyer*, 343 U.S. 579 (1952).

SUGGESTED RESOURCES

Calvi, James V., and Susan Coleman. *American Law and Legal Systems*, 6th ed. Upper Saddle River, N.J.: Prentice Hall, 2007. A systematic discussion of all the major types of law in the United States.

Hall, Kermit L., and Peter Karsten. *The Magic Mirror: Law in American History.* New York: Oxford University Press, 2008. A discussion of the historical interactions of law with events in the social and political realms.

Johnson, Conrad. *Philosophy of Law.* New York: Macmillan, 1993. A wide selection of readings about various philosophies of law, punishment, liberty, legal reasoning, and so on.

Sarat, Austin, ed. *The Social Organization of Law: Introductory Readings.* Los Angeles: Roxbury, 2004. A collection of readings on diverse topics such as the purpose of law, the dilemmas inherent in social organization, and the discretionary aspects of the judicial system.

Vago, Steven. *Law and Society*, 9th ed. Upper Saddle River, N.J.: Prentice Hall, 2009. A good summary of law and society issues in the United States, with an excellent comparative perspective on these issues.

Robert A. Carp, Ronald Stidham, and Kenneth L. Manning, *The State Courts,* (Washington, DC: CQ Press, 2010).

2. STATE JUDICIAL SYSTEMS

Even before the Articles of Confederation and the writing of the U.S. Constitution in 1787, the colonies, as sovereign entities, already had written constitutions, which provided for judicial oversight. The development of the organization and procedures of state court systems can therefore be traced from the colonial period.

HISTORICAL DEVELOPMENT OF STATE COURTS

No two states are exactly alike when it comes to the organization of courts. Each state is entirely free to adopt any organizational scheme it chooses, create as many courts as it wishes, name those courts whatever it pleases, and establish their jurisdiction as it sees fit. The organization of state courts, therefore, does not necessarily resemble the clear-cut three-tier system found at the federal level. In the federal system the trial courts are called district courts, and the appellate tribunals are known as circuit courts, but in well over a dozen states the circuit courts are known as *trial courts.* Several other states use the term *superior court* for their major trial courts. Perhaps the most bewildering situation is found in New York, where the major trial courts are known as *supreme courts.*

Although a great deal of confusion surrounds the organization of state courts, no doubt exists about their importance. Because statutory law is more extensive in the states than at the federal level, covering everything from the most basic personal relationships to the state's most important public policies, the state courts handle a wide variety of cases. One study of state supreme courts says that the main categories of cases include

> appeals in major felonies; state regulation of business and professions; a wide range of private economic disputes, including business contracts and real estate; wills, trusts, and estates; divorce, child custody, and child support; and personal injury suits involving automobile accidents, medical malpractice, job-related injuries, and the like.[1]

State courts also interpret their own state constitutions, which sometimes have broader protections for their citizens than are found in the federal constitution. In fact, "since the 1970s, state courts (particularly the highest courts of the states) have issued hundreds of opinions interpreting their constitutions to protect rights beyond the federal minima."[2] U.S. Supreme Court justice William Brennan, in an influential law review article published in 1977, is generally credited with encouraging state courts to interpret their own constitutions to provide greater protection of citizens' rights.[3] One study of this development, known as "new judicial federalism," found a dramatic increase in state courts' reliance on state declarations of rights in civil liberties cases during the latter part of the twentieth century.[4] Not surprisingly, then, the number of cases litigated annually in the state courts far exceeds those decided in the federal tribunals.

As colonists moved from England to settle in America, they naturally brought with them the various customs and traditions with which they were familiar. For this reason, American law borrowed heavily from English common law. Likewise, common law traditions became important factors in shaping the state court systems. Ohio and Pennsylvania still call their major trial courts the courts of common pleas, a title whose origin may be traced to England.

The Colonial Period

During the colonial period, political power was concentrated in the hands of the governor, who was appointed by the king of England. Because the governors performed executive, legislative, and judicial functions, an elaborate court system was not necessary. The courts of this period were simple institutions that borrowed their form from the English judiciary, but the colonists greatly simplified the English procedures to suit their own needs.

The lowest level of the colonial judiciary consisted of local judges called justices of the peace or **magistrates,** who were appointed by the colony's governor. At the next level in the system were the county courts, the general trial courts for the colonies. These courts "were at the heart of colonial government."[5] In addition to deciding cases, they performed some administrative functions. Appeals from all courts were taken to the highest level—the governor and his council. **Grand** and **petit juries** were also introduced during this period and remain prominent features of the state judicial systems.

By the early eighteenth century the legal profession had begun to change. Lawyers trained in the English Inns of Court became more numerous, and as a consequence colonial court procedures were slowly replaced by more sophisticated English common law. In addition, common commercial needs and a common language helped to make colonial and English legal practices more similar. As one judicial scholar notes, "In a relatively short time—between 1760 and 1820—a rather backward colonial legal framework was transformed into a very English common law system."[6]

Early State Courts

Following the American Revolution, the powers of the government were not only taken over by legislative bodies but also greatly reduced in scope. The former colonists were not eager to see the development of a large independent judiciary, given that many of them harbored a distrust of lawyers and the common law. The state legislatures carefully watched the courts and in some instances removed judges or abolished specific courts because of unpopular decisions. The basic structure of the state judiciaries, however, was not greatly altered.

Over time, a distrust of the judiciary developed as courts declared legislative actions unconstitutional. Conflicts between legislatures and judges, often stemming from opposing interests, became more prevalent. Legislators seemed more responsive to policies that favored debtors, whereas courts generally reflected the views of creditors. These differences were important, because "out of this conflict over legislative and judicial power … the courts gradually emerged as an independent political institution." [7]

Modern State Courts

From the Civil War to the early twenty-first century, the state courts confronted still other problems. Increasing industrialization and the rapid growth of urban areas created new types of legal disputes and resulted in longer and more complex court cases. The state court systems, largely fashioned to handle the problems of a rural agrarian society, were now faced with a crisis of backlogs as they struggled to adjust.

One typical response was to create new courts to handle the increased volume of cases. Courts were often simply piled on top of one another with overlapping jurisdictions. Another strategy was the addition of new courts, coupled with a careful specification of their jurisdiction in terms of geographic area. Still another response was to create specialized courts, such as small-claims courts, juvenile courts, and domestic relations courts, to handle one particular type of case.

The result of all this activity was a confusing array of courts, especially in the major urban areas, where growth tended to be more pronounced. One observer noted that

> each court was a separate entity; each had a judge and a staff. Such an organizational structure meant there was no way to shift cases from an overloaded court to one with little to do. In addition, each court produced political patronage jobs for the city political machines.[8]

The largely unplanned expansion of state and local courts to meet specific needs led to a situation many have referred to as fragmentation. A multiplicity of trial courts was only one aspect of fragmentation. Many of these courts had very narrow jurisdictions, but sometimes the jurisdictions overlapped, which meant that a case could be tried in a number of courts depending on the advantages each one offered. Court costs, court procedures, court delays, and the reputation of the judge all entered into the decision of which court to choose. A strict law-and-order district attorney prosecuting a criminal case might choose a court with a reputation for handing out stiff sentences. An attorney filing a civil suit on behalf of a client might seek a court known for its complex procedures to draw the other side into a confusing web of legal technicalities. Political considerations were also involved in the choice of a court. The justice of the peace courts were especially political because many of them operated on a fee basis. Justices of the peace (J. P.s) were often willing to trade favorable decisions for court business. The initials J. P. were often said to stand for "Justice for the Plaintiff."[9]

In the early twentieth century people began to speak out against the fragmentation in the state court systems. The program of reforms that emerged in response is generally known as the court unification movement. The first well-known legal scholar to speak out in favor of court unification was Roscoe Pound, dean of Harvard Law School.[10] Pound and others called for the consolidation of trial courts into a single set of courts or two sets of courts, one to hear major cases and one to hear minor cases.

These ideas have elicited a good deal of opposition. Many trial lawyers who are in court almost daily become accustomed to existing court organization and therefore are opposed to change. Knowledge of the local courts is the key to their success, so they naturally are not eager to try cases in strange new courts.

Also, judges and other personnel associated with the courts are sometimes opposed to reform. Their opposition often grows out of fear of being transferred to new courts, having to learn new procedures, or having to decide cases outside their area of specialization. Nonlawyer judges, such as justices of the peace, often oppose court reform because they view it as a threat to their jobs. The court unification movement, then, has not been as successful as many would like, although proponents of court reform have secured victories in some states.

STATE COURT ORGANIZATION

Some states have moved closer to a unified court system, whereas others still operate with a bewildering complex of courts with overlapping jurisdiction. The California court system, shown in Figure 2-1, is an example of a simplified state court system. Like the federal court system, it consists of one level of trial courts, regional courts of appeals, and one high court.

The New York court system, on the other hand, provides an example of a state with a complex network of courts. A look at Figure 2-2 indicates that there are ten trial courts, two appellate courts, and one high court in the state. These courts are staffed by more than 3,500 judicial officials known in different courts as judges, justices, or surrogates.

Most states, falling somewhere between the two extremes illustrated in Figures 2–1 and 2–2, are divided into four general categories or levels: trial courts of limited jurisdiction, trial courts of general jurisdiction, intermediate appellate courts, and courts of last resort.

Figure **2-1** Court System of California

Supreme Court COLR
7 justices sit en banc A

CSP Case Types:
- Mandatory jurisdiction in capital criminal, disciplinary cases.
- Discretionary jurisdiction in civil, noncapital criminal, administrative agency, juvenile, original proceeding, interlocutory decision cases.

↑

Courts of Appeal (6 courts/districts) IAC
105 justices sit in panels A

CSP Case Types:
- Mandatory jurisdiction in civil, noncapital criminal, administrative agency, juvenile cases.
- Discretionary jurisdiction in administrative agency, original proceeding, interlocutory decision cases.

↑

Superior Court (58 counties) GJC
1,548 judges, 423 commissioners and referees A
Jury trials except in appeals, domestic relations, and juvenile cases

CSP Case Types:
- Tort, contract, real property ($25,000 – no maximum), miscellaneous civil. Exclusive small claims (up to $5,000), probate/estate, mental health, civil appeals. [Limited jurisdiction: tort, contract, real property ($ - $25,000).]
- Exclusive domestic relations.
- Exclusive criminal.
- Exclusive juvenile.
- Exclusive traffic\other violations.

Legend
(bold rounded box) = Appellate level
(thin rounded box) = Trial level
COLR = Court of Last Resort
IAC = Intermediate Appellate Court
GJC = General Jurisdiction Court
LJC = Limited Jurisdiction Court
A = Appeal from Admin. Agency
↑ = Route of appeal

SOURCE: National Center for State Courts. www.ncsconlinc.org/D_RescarcrL/Ct_Struct/statc_irLc.asp?STATE=CA. Reprinted by permission.

NOTE: CSP indicates that these case types are included in the Court Statistics Project of the National Center for State Courts.

Figure **2-2** Court System of New York

(Court structure as of Calendar Year 2007)

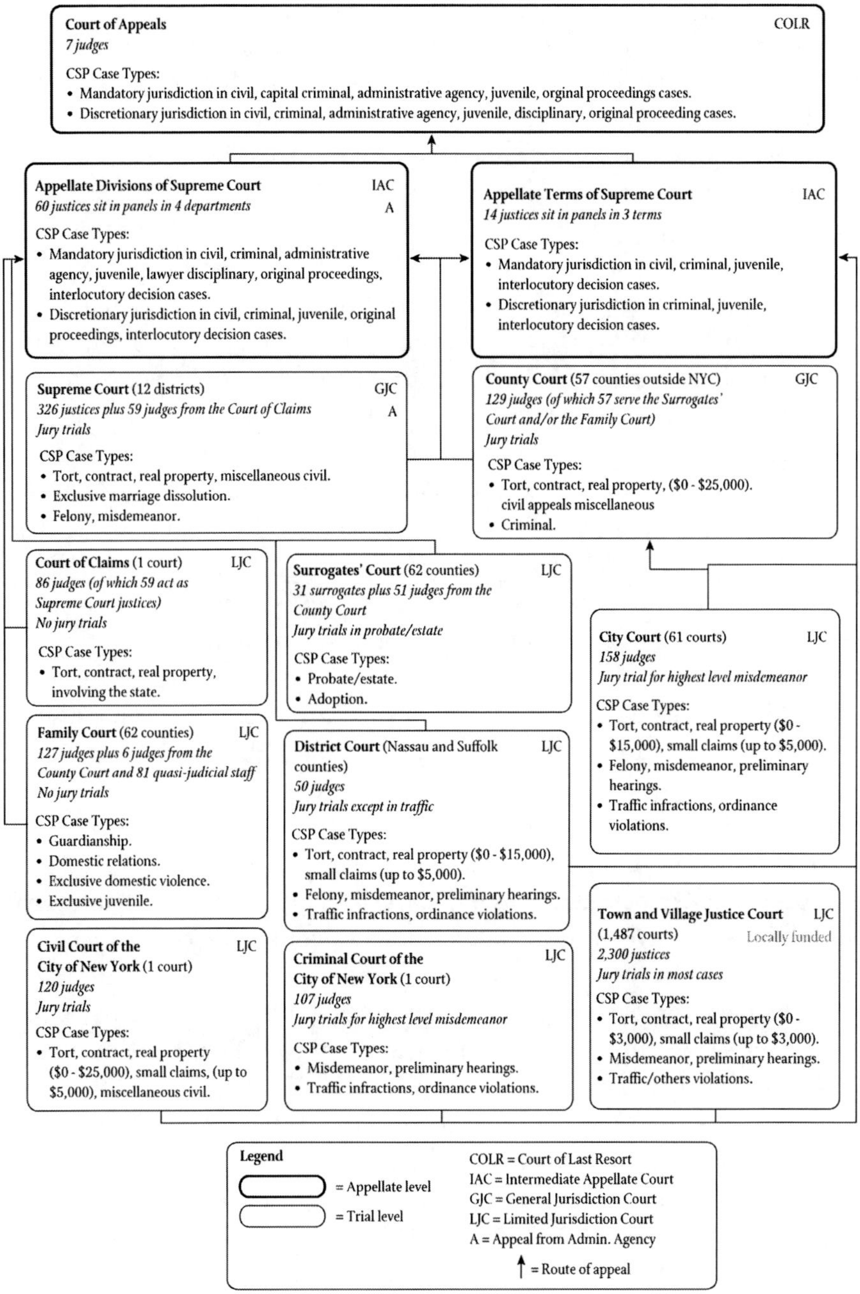

SOURCE: National Center for State Courrs. www.ncsconline.org/D_Reserch/Ct_Strutt/include/NY_P.Pdf. Reprinted by permission.

NOTE: CSP indicates that case types are included in the Court Statistics Project of the National Center for State Courts.

Trial Courts of Limited Jurisdiction

Trial courts of limited jurisdiction handle the bulk of litigation in this country each year and constitute about 85 percent of all courts in the United States.[11] They have a variety of names: among the most common are justice of the peace courts, magistrate courts, municipal courts, city courts, county courts, juvenile courts, domestic relations courts, and metropolitan courts.

The jurisdiction of these courts is limited to minor cases. In criminal matters, for example, state courts deal with three levels of violations: infractions (the least serious), misdemeanors (more serious), and felonies (the most serious). Trial courts of limited jurisdiction typically handle infractions and misdemeanors. They may impose only limited fines (usually no more than $1,000) and jail sentences (generally no more than one year). In civil cases these courts are usually limited to disputes under a certain amount, such as $3,000. In addition, these types of courts are often limited to certain kinds of matters: traffic violations, domestic relations, or cases involving juveniles, for example. Another difference is that in many instances these limited courts are not courts of record. Because their proceedings are not recorded, appeals of their decisions usually go to a trial court of general jurisdiction for what is known as a **trial de novo** (new trial).

New York is one of about thirty states that rely on a large number of local trial courts of limited jurisdiction to dispense justice at the lowest level. One such group, the nearly 1,500 Town and Village Justice courts, has more than 2,000 judges spread throughout all areas of the state except New York City.

In a series of in-depth articles published in the *New York Times* in 2006, William Glaberson offers some startling facts about these locally funded courts, which are staffed by judges popularly elected to four-year terms. First, he reports that nearly three-quarters of the judges who preside over these courts are not lawyers but truck drivers, sewer workers, and laborers who have a scant grasp of the most basic legal principles. Some never finished high school and at least one never got further than grade school. In fact, Glaberson claims that New York demands more training for licensed manicurists and hair stylists than for this group of elected judges. Second, Glaberson points out that these courts suffer from a serious lack of resources because they are funded by local levels of government rather than the state legislature. Because of this lack of resources, the judges must often hold court in tiny offices or basement rooms without a judge's bench or a jury box, rather than in real courtrooms. Furthermore, there is often no money available to employ court reporters or other clerical support staff. Therefore, protocol in some of these courts dictates that the public is not admitted, witnesses are not sworn to tell the truth, and no word-for-word record of the proceedings is created. Judges are simply not required to make transcripts or tape recordings of what happens in the court.

Even though the judges presiding over the Town and Village Justice courts are generally nonlawyers with only six days of training classes at the start of their tenure and a twelve-hour refresher course each year thereafter, they perform some important duties. In the criminal area they can set **bail,** hold preliminary hearings in **felony** cases, and conduct trials in misdemeanor cases. On the civil side, they can preside over cases involving claims of up to $3,000 and landlord-tenant disputes with no dollar limit.[12]

Trial Courts of General Jurisdiction

Most states have one set of major trial courts that handle the more serious criminal and civil cases. In addition, in many states, special categories—such as juvenile criminal offenses, domestic relations cases, and probate cases—are under the jurisdiction of the general trial courts.

In the majority of states these courts also have an appellate function. They hear appeals in certain types of cases that originate in trial courts of limited jurisdiction. These appeals are often heard in a trial de novo or tried again in the court of general jurisdiction.

General trial courts are usually divided into judicial districts or circuits. Although the practice varies from state to state, the general rule is to use existing political boundaries such as a county or a group of counties in establishing the district or circuit. In rural areas the judge may ride from one town to another within the district or circuit to hold court in different parts of the territory according to a fixed schedule. In urban areas judges hold court in a prescribed place throughout the year. In larger counties the group of judges may be divided into specializations. Some may hear only civil cases; others try criminal cases exclusively.

The courts at this level have a variety of names. The most common are district, circuit, and superior. As noted earlier, Ohio and Pennsylvania still cling to the title "court of common pleas." New York is undoubtedly the most confusing of all; its trial court of general jurisdiction is called the supreme court (see Figure 2-2). The judges at this level are required by law in all states to have law degrees. These courts also maintain clerical help because they are courts of record. In other words, a degree of professionalism is evident at this level that is often lacking in the trial courts of limited jurisdiction.

Intermediate Appellate Courts

The intermediate appellate courts are relative newcomers to the state judicial scene. Only thirteen such courts existed in 1911, whereas forty states now have them. Their basic purpose is to relieve the workload of the state's highest court.

In most instances they are called courts of appeals, although other names are occasionally used. Most states have one **court of appeals** with statewide jurisdiction. Other states, such as California, Ohio, and Texas, have created regional appellate courts to hear appeals from trial courts in a specific area. Alabama and Tennessee have separate intermediate appellate courts for civil and criminal cases.

The names of these intermediate appellate courts vary. The size of intermediate courts also varies from state to state. The court of appeals in Alaska has only three judges. At the other extreme, California has 105 courts of appeals judges.[13] In some states the intermediate appeals courts sit **en banc,** whereas in other states they sit in permanent or rotating panels.

Generally speaking, the jurisdiction of intermediate appellate courts is mandatory because Americans hold to the view that parties in a case are entitled to at least one appeal. In numerous instances, these are the courts of last resort for litigants in the state court system.

Courts of Last Resort

Every state has a court of last resort. Oklahoma and Texas have two highest courts. Both states have a supreme court with jurisdiction limited to appeals in civil cases and a court of criminal appeals for criminal cases. Most states call their highest courts supreme courts; other designations are the court of appeals (Maryland and New York), the supreme judicial court (Maine and Massachusetts), and the supreme court of appeals (West Virginia).

The courts of last resort range in size from five to nine judges (called justices in some states). They typically sit en banc and usually, although not necessarily, in the state capital.

The highest courts have jurisdiction in matters pertaining to state law and are the final arbiters in such matters. In states that have intermediate appellate courts, the supreme court's cases come primarily from these mid-level courts. In this situation the high court typically is allowed to exercise discretion in deciding which cases to review. It is therefore likely to devote more time to cases that deal with the important policy issues of the state. In the absence of an intermediate court of appeals, cases generally go to the state's highest court on a mandatory review basis. This arrangement is likely to create an error correction function for the court of last resort in routine cases and to reduce its opportunities for policymaking.[14]

In most instances, the state courts of last resort resemble the U.S. Supreme Court in that the justices have a good deal of discretion in determining which cases to hear. Most state supreme courts also follow procedures similar to those of the U.S. Supreme Court. When a case is accepted for review, the opposing parties file written briefs and later present oral arguments. Amicus curiae briefs are also filed quite frequently in states such as California, Illinois, Michigan, Oklahoma, Pennsylvania, and Wisconsin.[15] After reaching a decision, the judges issue written opinions explaining that decision.

Juvenile Courts

Even the most casual reading of a daily newspaper or the viewing of a nightly news broadcast tells us that Americans are becoming more concerned about the handling of cases involving juveniles. Not surprisingly, states have responded to the problem in a variety of ways.[16] Some have established a statewide network of courts specifically to handle matters involving juveniles. They are commonly called juvenile courts or family courts. Georgia has juvenile courts throughout the state. Rhode Island and South Carolina provide good examples of another approach. These two states have family courts, which handle domestic relations matters as well as those involving juveniles. Still other states have juvenile courts or family courts or both in limited areas. In Colorado, there is a juvenile court for Denver. Louisiana has created four juvenile courts for the state and one family court in East Baton Rouge Parish.

The most common approach is to give one or more of the state's limited or general trial courts jurisdiction to handle situations involving juveniles. In Alabama the circuit courts (trial courts of general jurisdiction) deal with juvenile matters. In Virginia, however, juvenile jurisdiction is lodged in trial courts of limited jurisdiction—the district courts.

Finally, some states apportion juvenile jurisdiction among more than one court. Recall the juvenile court in Denver. No one imagines that problems among juveniles in Colorado are limited to the city of Denver. Instead, the state has given jurisdiction over juveniles to district courts (general trial courts) in areas other than Denver.

As might be expected, the states vary in determining when jurisdiction belongs to an adult court. States set a standard age at which defendants are tried in an adult court. In addition, many states require that younger offenders be tried in an adult court if special circumstances are present. In Illinois the standard age at which juvenile jurisdiction transfers to adult courts is seventeen. The age limit drops to fifteen, however, for first-degree murder, aggravated criminal sexual assault, armed robbery, robbery with a firearm, and unlawful use of weapons on school grounds.

NORM ENFORCEMENT IN STATE COURTS

Norm enforcement is closely tied to the administration of justice and the maintenance of societal norms embodied in statutes, administrative regulations, and community traditions. Because statutory law is so extensive in the states, it is only natural that much of the work of state courts, especially in trial courts of limited jurisdiction, involves norm enforcement rather than policymaking. According to one recent study, describing the work of state judges,

> Some of their workload is administrative (for example, the probating of wills). Another part involves conflict resolution (for example, deciding which party is correct in contested divorce settlements and property disputes). And still another area of responsibility includes the criminal prosecution and appeals process.[17]

The handling of criminal cases in the state courts is especially important because "anyone who looks at the local news, reads the newspapers, listens to talk shows, or gossips with the neighbors knows that crime, criminal justice, and criminal courts attract nearly everyone's enduring interest and morbid fascination." [18] Even though similar rules and processes are used to prosecute criminal cases throughout the United States, careful observers tell us that there are also notable differences from one courthouse to another. How do we explain these differences, which exist not only among courts in different cities but also among different judges' courtrooms in the same city?

One plausible explanation, prominent in the social science literature, notes that the culture of a community, that is, its shared beliefs and attitudes, influences how its members behave. These shared beliefs and attitudes may help explain the actions of entire nations or smaller communities within a nation. Many legal scholars argue that a local legal culture—norms shared by members of the local court community—determines how criminal cases will be prosecuted in a particular courtroom.[19]

The values and norms shared by judges, attorneys, clerks, bailiffs, probation officers, and others who work in the court system influence court operations in three important ways.[20] First, they help participants distinguish between "our" court and other courts. Attorneys and judges will often boast that they process cases more efficiently than other courts within the city or state. Second, norms tell members of a court community how they should treat one another. Third, the norms describe how cases should be processed in a particular court. In short, the local legal culture helps us understand why different courts handle things differently, even though the formal rules of criminal procedure are basically the same.

THE COURTROOM WORK GROUP

Implicit in the notion of courts as communities is the belief that courts are permanent organizations rather than occasional gatherings of strangers who resolve a particular conflict and then go their separate ways.[21] The most visible members of this permanent organization are judges, prosecutors, and defense attorneys. Commonly referred to as the courtroom work group, each is generally associated with a specific function. Prosecutors push for convictions of those accused of criminal offenses against the government; defense attorneys seek acquittals for their clients; and judges serve as neutral arbiters to guarantee a fair trial. In reality, members of the courtroom work group share certain values and goals and are not the fierce adversaries that many Americans imagine. Cooperation among judges, prosecutors, and defense attorneys is the norm.

The most important goal of the courtroom work group is to handle cases expeditiously. Judges and prosecutors are interested in disposing of cases quickly, to present a picture of accomplishment and efficiency. Because private defense attorneys need to handle a large volume of cases, resolving cases quickly works to their advantage, too. Public defenders seek quick dispositions simply because they generally lack adequate resources to handle their caseloads.

A second important goal of the courtroom work group is to maintain group cohesion. Conflict among the members makes work more difficult and interferes with the expeditious handling of cases. Therefore, the work group stresses cooperation and censures those who violate this norm.

Finally, the courtroom work group is interested in reducing or controlling uncertainty. In practice, this means that all members of the group strive to avoid trials. Trials, especially jury trials, produce a great deal of uncertainty, given that they require substantial investments of time and effort without any reasonable guarantee of a desirable outcome.

To attain the goals of handling cases expeditiously, maintaining group cohesion, and reducing uncertainty, work group members use several techniques. Although unilateral decisions and adversary proceedings occur, negotiation is the most commonly used technique in criminal courtrooms. The members negotiate on a variety of issues—continuances, hearing dates, and exchange of information, among other matters. Without a doubt, however, plea bargaining is the most heavily publicized subject of negotiation among members of the courtroom work group.

ADMINISTRATIVE HEARINGS IN THE STATES

For at least the last half century there has been a movement in the United States, at both the national and state levels, to separate agency hearings from their regulation and enforcement functions. The idea is that an agency should not be "the policeman, prosecutor, judge and jury of its own action." [22] To avoid this problem more than twenty states have created central panels of administrative law judges to conduct hearings. These judges are independent of the agencies for which they hold hearings.

Oregon provides an interesting and informative case study of this process in action.[23] Before 2000 Oregon, along with a number of other states, permitted hearing officers within the regulating agency to hear complaints by citizens and businesses who disputed the agency's action.

That changed when the Oregon legislature created the Office of Administrative Hearings (OAH) in 1999 and it began operating in 2000. Today the OAH has 119 permanent employees, including 65 administrative law judges, and is headed by a chief administrative law judge. According to OAH's Web site, the administrative law judges hold more than 30,000 hearings per year for about seventy state agencies. That number represents 90 percent or more of all the contested orders issued by agencies in Oregon.

POLICYMAKING IN STATE COURTS

State courts do more than simply enforce norms. There are also opportunities to engage in shaping policies in the state. One example of policymaking by state high courts involves the vastly unequal amounts spent in school districts within a state. After the U.S. Supreme Court held in *San Antonio Independent School District v. Rodriguez* that different spending patterns in poor and wealthy school districts within a state do not violate equal protection rights under the U.S. Constitution,[24] a number of legal challenges were mounted in state courts, arguing that unequal educational opportunities violate various clauses in state constitutions. This strategy has proven successful. One observer notes that

> state supreme courts in more than half the states have held that reliance on local property-tax revenues to fund public schools violates the right to a free public education contained in their respective state constitutions.[25]

Gay and lesbian rights have also fared better in the hands of state judges than in federal tribunals. The Georgia Supreme Court overturned the state's antisodomy law under the privacy provisions of the Georgia Constitution, even though the same law had been upheld in 1986 by the U.S. Supreme Court *(Bowers v. Hardwick).*[26]

Same-sex marriages, civil unions, and domestic partnerships have also been heavily contested in state courts. New Hampshire became the sixth state to allow same-sex couples to marry when its state legislature passed a law permitting such unions in June 2009. The new law took effect in January 2010.[27] New Hampshire's action solidified New England as the center of the same-sex marriage movement. Vermont legalized same-sex marriages in 2009. Maine first legalized same-sex marriages in spring 2009, but the voters repealed that state's law some six months later, in November. Connecticut, Massachusetts, and Iowa allowed same-sex marriages after the high courts in those states ruled it unconstitutional to deny gay couples the right to marry.[28]

Perhaps no state's courts have gained more notoriety than California's in grappling with the issue of same-sex marriage. In 2004, six separate cases were filed by supporters and opponents of same-sex marriage. They were eventually consolidated as *In re Marriage Cases* and heard by a superior court judge in San Francisco. This court held that California statutes limiting marriage to opposite-sex couples were unconstitutional, but a three-judge panel of the California Court of Appeals overturned the decision.[29]

The case next moved to the California Supreme Court. Many in the state were shocked when that court announced on May 15, 2008, that it was striking down California's existing statutes limiting marriage to opposite-sex couples.[30]

Although many hailed the court's decision, others sought to overturn it by amending the California Constitution and reinstating the principle that only opposite-sex couples could legally marry in the state. Supporters of the amendment were able to get an initiative to that effect on the ballot in the November 2008 election. Proposition 8, as the initiative was known, was approved by a majority of the voters.

Undaunted, supporters of same-sex marriage mounted another court challenge. Their hopes were dashed, however, when the California Supreme Court ruled on May 26, 2009, that their objections were without merit. California once again joined the list of states limiting marriage to opposite-sex couples. There was some solace for supporters of same-sex marriage, however. The court upheld the validity of same-sex marriages previously performed in California.[31]

Same-sex relationships may also be protected as domestic partnerships and civil unions, but the availability and rights of these alternatives vary greatly. Domestic partnerships have no federal protections. Protections such as health care, hospital visitations, and the right to meet with a nonbiological child's teacher are available through domestic partnership registries in several states and cities.[32] Civil unions, like domestic partnerships, have no federal protections even though same-sex couples may have access to state benefits.

As these examples of judicial activity concerning same-sex marriages, domestic partnerships, and civil unions illustrate, state court judges possess important tools that permit them to expand the rights of state citizens.[33] Whether state judges are willing and politically able to do so is a different matter. Many state judges are **conservative** and simply not inclined to engage in overt policymaking. Moreover, the political and legal climate in the state may work against an active policymaking agenda. In short, a combination of ideology, **judicial role,** interpretation, and political pressures may dictate that state high court judges not venture far from the status quo.[34]

INNOVATION IN STATE COURTS

Given the wide variety of problems facing state courts and the ever-present fights over scarce budget resources, it is not surprising that a substantial amount of innovation has occurred in the state judiciaries. As noted earlier, some states have created specialized courts to handle particular types of case, ranging from water courts (which resolve legal disputes over water rights in states with scarce water supplies) and probate courts to others dealing with domestic relations, small claims, and juveniles.

Over the past few decades court-connected **alternative dispute resolution (ADR)** has spread throughout the country as a way to avoid lengthy court involvement in certain types of cases. According to the National Center for State Courts, every state now has some type of court-connected ADR at some level.[35]

Innovations have also been made in the way cases are placed on a court's docket, so that the less complicated cases may be resolved more quickly and not be delayed while the court hears more complicated cases. Changes in the courts' calendar systems have made it easier to track cases and keep all involved parties up-to-date on the status of the case. Increasing the use of technology has also been a priority in many state court systems, as computer records have largely replaced paper trails in everything from the filing of cases to the publication of final decisions. Perhaps more important, state judicial systems have begun to examine the very reasons for the existence of courts. It is to that issue that we next turn our attention.

By the latter part of the twentieth century some state courts were changing from adversarial arenas to problem-solving courts that focused on the underlying behavior of criminal defendants. Drawing on a concept known as therapeutic jurisprudence, these new problem-solving courts were expected to include services along with judicial case processing.[36]

Perhaps the best-known examples are the drug courts that now exist in many states. Often referred to as drug treatment courts, they emphasize therapeutic measures to reduce recidivism and generally include essential elements such as immediate intervention, nonad-versary adjudication, hands-on judicial involvement, treatment programs with clear rules and structured goals, and a team approach that brings together judges, prosecutors, defense attorneys, treatment providers, and corrections personnel.[37]

Other types of problem-solving courts have also become popular, among them mental health courts, teen courts, domestic violence courts, DWI courts, and reentry courts. Some are permanent courts, while others are pilot or model programs. Still others exist as specialized dockets of established courts. Whatever the specific approach, it is clear that the state courts are willing and imaginative innovators.

ADMINISTRATIVE AND STAFF SUPPORT IN THE STATE JUDICIARY

The daily operation of the federal courts requires the efforts of many individuals and organizations. This is no less true for the state court systems.

Magistrates

State **magistrates,** who may also be known in some states as commissioners or referees, are often used to perform some of the work in the early stages of civil and criminal case processing. In this way they are similar to U.S. magistrate judges. In some jurisdictions they hold bond hearings and conduct preliminary investigations in criminal cases. They are also authorized in some states to make decisions in minor cases. In North Carolina, for example, the magistrates who lend support to the state's district courts may accept guilty pleas on certain traffic violations as well as preside over small-claims cases.

Law Clerks

In the state courts, law clerks are likely to be found, if at all, in the intermediate appellate courts and courts of last resort. Most state trial courts do not utilize law clerks, and they are practically unheard of in local trial courts of limited jurisdiction. As at the national level, some law clerks work for individual judges, and others function as staff attorneys for an entire court.

Administrative Office of the Courts

Every state now has an administrative office of the courts or a similarly titled agency that performs a variety of administrative tasks for its court system. The size of the administrative office and its operating budget vary from state to state, so that some of these agencies perform more tasks than others. Among the duties more commonly associated with administrative offices are budget preparation, data processing, facility management, judicial education, public information, research, and personnel management. A number of administrative offices have total or partial responsibility for one or more of these tasks. In some states still other jobs are assigned to administrative offices. Juvenile and adult probation are the responsibility of administrative offices in a few states, as is ADR.

Court Clerks and Court Administrators

The clerk of the court has traditionally handled the day-to-day routines of the court, which includes making courtroom arrangements, keeping records of case proceedings, preparing orders and judgments resulting from court actions, collecting court fines and fees, and disbursing judicial monies. In the majority of states these officials are elected and may be referred to by other titles.

In many areas the traditional court clerks have been replaced by court administrators.

In contrast to the court clerk, who managed the operations of a specific courtroom, the modern court administrator may assist a presiding judge in running the entire courthouse. Even more broadly, in some states the administrator may work for a statewide organization that oversees all the state court systems at the city or county level.

STATE COURT WORKLOAD

The lion's share of the nation's judicial business exists at the state, not the national, level. That federal judges adjudicate several hundred thousand cases in a year is impressive; that state courts handle several *million* in a year is overwhelming. Although justice of the peace and magistrate courts at the state level handle relatively minor matters, a number of multimillion-dollar judgments in civil cases are annually awarded by ordinary state trial court juries.

Reliable data on the number of cases filed in the state courts are somewhat difficult to come by. Record-keeping is much better in some states than others, and some of the lower level courts, which are sometimes not courts of record, often greatly vary. Nonetheless, the National Center for State Courts does an excellent job of tracking the figures for the states' trial courts.

The first part of Figure 2-3 compares the number of cases entering the nation's state courts between 1997 and 2006. The number stood at slightly more than 90 million cases in 1997. That number had increased by 2006 to nearly 100 million cases, an increase of 10 percent.

Figure **2-3**

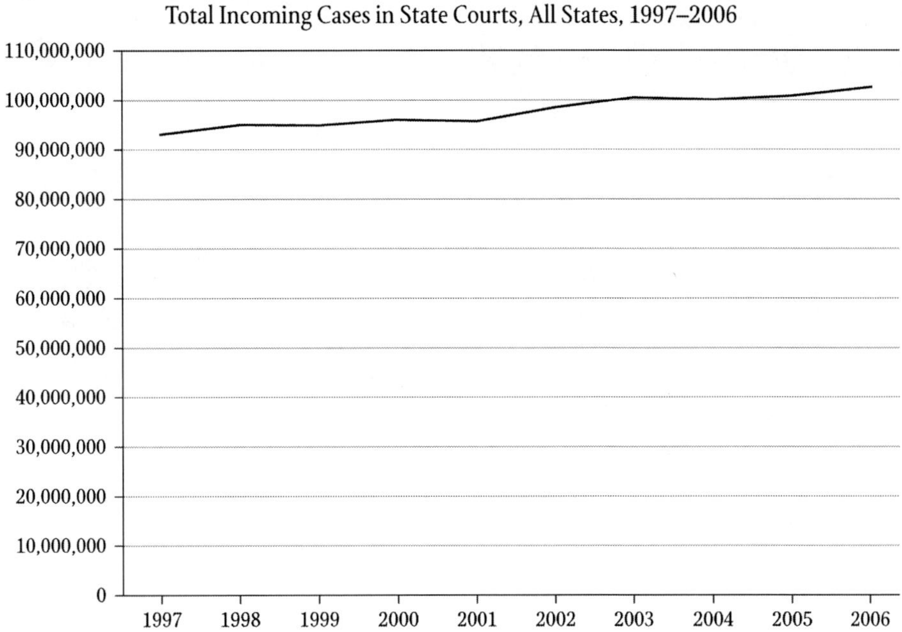

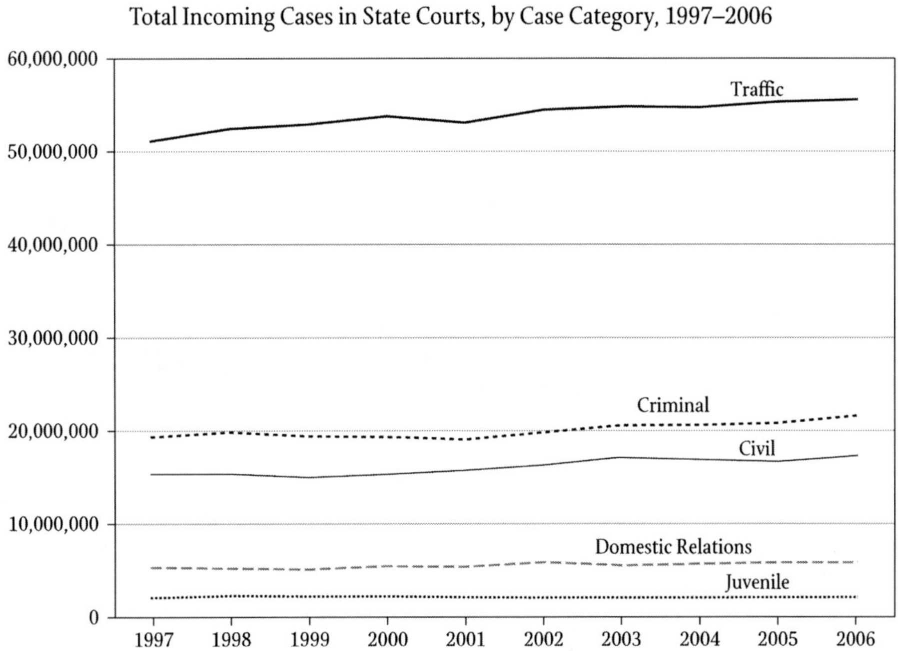

SOURCE: National Center for Stale Courts, "Examining the Work of Stale Courts 2007." www.ncsconline.Org/D_Research/csp/2UO7_files/Examining%20Final%20-%202007%20-%204%20-%20Overview.pdf Reprinted by permission.

The second part of Figure 2-3 provides a bit more detail about the cases entering state courts by breaking them down by categories. Traffic cases, which far outnumber the other categories, increased by 9 percent between 1997 and 2006. Incoming criminal and civil cases increased over the same ten-year period by 12 percent and 13 percent, respectively. Domestic relations cases climbed by 10 percent from 1997 to 2006. Juvenile cases entering the state courts during the comparable time period remained flat, however.

Total appellate filings in the state courts over the ten-year period from 1997 to 2006 are shown in Figure 2-4. The number of cases filed in state appellate courts declined 4 percent, from about 300,000 cases in 1997 to about 288,000 cases in 2006.

Figure **2-4** Total Appellate Filings, 1997–2006

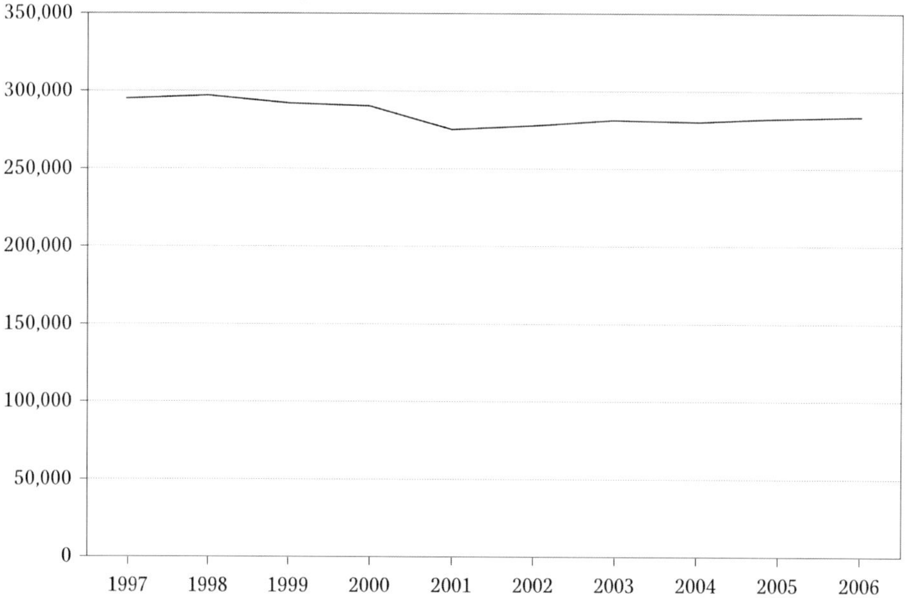

SOURCE: National Center for Slate Courts, "Examining the Work of State Courts, 2007." Reprinted by permission.

SUMMARY

In this chapter we offered a brief historical review of the development of state judicial systems. Although no two state court systems are alike, they all have four basic levels: trial courts of limited jurisdiction, trial courts of general jurisdiction, intermediate appellate courts, and courts of last resort. We examined the work done at each of these four levels. Our discussion also included a look at the handling of juvenile cases within the states. In addition, we discussed norm enforcement, policymaking by state courts in the context of new judicial federalism, and innovation, primarily in the context of problem-solving courts.

In discussing administrative assistance for the state courts, our review centered on administrative offices of the courts, law clerks, court clerks and court administrators, and magistrates. We concluded with a brief look at the workload of the state trial and appellate courts.

FURTHER THOUGHT AND DISCUSSION QUESTIONS

1. Does a unified court system provide the best way for state courts to handle their legal issues?
2. Why are state courts not as commonly recognized for their policymaking activities as the federal courts?
3. What conclusions may be drawn from an examination of state court caseload statistics?

Notes

1. Henry R. Glick, "Policy Making and State Supreme Courts," in *The American Courts: A Critical Assessment,* ed. John B. Gates and Charles A. Johnson (Washington, D.C.: CQ Press, 1991), 88.
2. Michael E. Solomine and James L. Walker, *Respecting State Courts: The Inevitability of Judicial Federalism* (Westport, Conn.: Greenwood Press, 1999), 89.
3. William J. Brennan Jr., "State Constitutions and the Protection of Individual Rights," *Harvard Law Review* 90 (1977): 489–504.
4. See G. Alan Tarr, *Understanding State Constitutions* (Princeton, N.J.: Princeton University Press, 1998), 165.
5. Lawrence M. Friedman, *A History of American Law,* 2nd ed. (New York: Simon and Schuster, 1985), 43.
6. Harry P. Stumpf, *American Judicial Politics,* 2nd ed. (Upper Saddle River, N.J.: Prentice Hall, 1998), 74.
7. David W. Neubauer, *America's Courts and the Criminal Justice System,* 2nd ed. (Monterey, Calif.: Brooks/Cole, 1984), 37.
8. Ibid., 38.
9. Henry J. Abraham, *The Judicial Process,* 6th ed. (New York: Oxford University Press, 1993), 138.
10. See Roscoe Pound, "The Causes of Popular Dissatisfaction with the Administration of Justice," *Journal of the American Judicature Society* 20 (1937): 178–187.
11. Stumpf, *American Judicial Politics,* 75.
12. All the examples included here are taken from William Glaberson, "In Tiny Courts of N.Y., Abuses of Law and Power," *New York Times,* September 25, 2006, available online at www.nytimes.com/2006/09/25/nyregion/25courts.html?_r=1&pagewanted=print. The second article in the series is "Small-Town Justice, With Trial and Error," *New York Times,* September 26, 2006, available online at www.nytimes.com/2006/09/26/nyregion/26courts.html?pagewanted=print. The third article is "How a Reviled Court System Has Outlasted Critics," *New York Times,* September 27, 2006, available online at www.nytimes.com/2006/09/27/nyregion/27courts.html?pagewanted=print.
13. See National Center for State Courts, *State Court Caseload Statistics, 2007,* available online at ncsconline.org.

14. For a study of the roles of state courts of last resort in these structural settings, see Burton M. Atkins and Henry R. Glick, "Environmental and Structural Variables as Determinants of Issues in State Courts of Last Resort," *American Journal of Political Science* 20 (February 1976): 97–115.

15. See Paul Brace and Melinda Gann Hall, "Comparing Courts Using the American States," *Judicature* 83 (March-April 2000): 264–265.

16. Our discussion of the various approaches to handling juvenile matters in the states is based on material found in National Center for State Courts, *State Court Caseload Statistics, 2007,* available online at ncsconline.org.

17. Thad L. Beyle, ed., *State and Local Government, 2002–2003* (Washington, D.C.: CQ Press, 2003), 141.

18. James Eisenstein, Roy B. Flemming, and Peter F. Nardulli, *The Contours of Justice: Communities and Their Courts* (Boston: Little, Brown, 1988), 3.

19. For an important study of the influence of local legal culture in nine medium-size criminal courts in three states, see ibid.

20. Our discussion of these influences is based on George F. Cole, Marc G. Gertz, and Amy Bunger, *The Criminal Justice System: Politics and Policies,* 9th ed. (Belmont, Calif.: Wadsworth/Thomson, 2004), 253–254.

21. See James Eisenstein and Herbert Jacob, *Felony Justice* (Boston: Little, Brown, 1977). Our discussion of the concept of the courtroom work group relies heavily on Eisenstein and Jacob's discussion.

22. State of Oregon, Office of Administrative Hearings, at www.oregon.gov/OAH/The_OAH2.shtml.

23. Ibid. Also see www.oregon.gov/OAH/about_us.shtml. Our discussion is drawn from these two sources.

24. *San Antonio Independent School District v. Rodriguez,* 411 U.S. 1 (1973).

25. Brian L. Porto, *May It Please the Court* (New York: Longman, 2001), 264. A list of some of the better-known cases and an excerpt from one of them may also be found in this book.

26. *Bowers v. Hardwick,* 478 U.S. 186 (1986). See Lee Epstein and Thomas G. Walker, *Constitutional Law for a Changing America: Rights, Liberties, and Justice,* 7th ed. (Washington, D.C.: CQ Press, 2010), 420–422.

27. Daniel Barrick, "Gay Marriage Becomes Law," *Concord Monitor,* June 4, 2009, available online at www.concordmonitor.com.

28. Ibid.

29. *In re Marriage Cases,* available online at www.courtinfo.ca.gov/opinions/documents/A110449.pdf.

30. *In re Marriage Cases,* available online at www.courtinfo.ca.gov/opinions/archives/S147999.pdf.

31. See "News Release: Supreme Court Rejects Challenges to Prop. 8, but Finds Existing Marriages of Same-Sex Couples Valid," available online at www.courtinfo.ca.gov/presscenter/newsreleases/NR29-09.pdf.

32. See Tracy Peters, Neal Kauder, Chuck Campbell, and Carol Flango, *Future Trends in State Courts 2005* (Williamsburg, Va.: National Center for State Courts, 2005), 121. For an informative summary of rights afforded gay couples in the various states, see Factbox: U.S. Laws on Gay Marriage, Civil Unions, available online at www.reuters.com.

33. For a good summary of state supreme court policymaking activities see Stumpf, *American Judicial Politics,* 367–376.

34. See the discussion in Albert P. Melone and Allan Karnes, *The American Legal System: Foundations, Processes, and Norms* (Los Angeles: Roxbury, 2003), 119–120.

35. See the National Center for State Courts at www.ncsconline.org/WC/Publications/ADR/default.htm for information on the various programs in the different states.

36. See Randy Monchick, Anna Scheyett, and Jane Pfeiffer, "Drug Court Case Management: Role, Function, and Utility," available online at www.ojp.usdoj.gov/BJA/pdf/Drug_Court_Case_

Management.pdf. Although this article focuses specifically on drug courts, it also provides an excellent overview of the general principles of therapeutic jurisprudence.

37. Ibid.

SUGGESTED RESOURCES

Bureau of Justice Statistics. Available online at www.ojp.usdoj.gov/bjs/courts.htm. Important information and statistics on state courts.

Eisenstein, James, Roy B. Flemming, and Peter F. Nardulli. *The Contours of Justice: Communities and Their Courts.* Boston: Little, Brown, 1988. Excellent study of the processing of felony criminal cases in nine medium-size courts in three states. The study examines how different courts in different communities incorporate local norms into court procedures.

FindLaw. Available online at www.findlaw.com. Useful information about individual state courts and state laws.

National Center for State Courts. Available online at www.ncsconline.org. Excellent source of information and statistics related to the work of state courts. Also contains links to individual state court systems.

National Drug Court Institute. Available online at www.ndci.org. Institute distributes information about drug court programs and training for officials.

Solomine, Michael E., and James L. Walker. *Respecting State Courts: The Inevitability of Judicial Federalism.* Westport, Conn.: Greenwood Press, 1999. A good book about the relationship between the federal and state court systems.

State Justice Institute. Available online at www.statejustice.org. Established to award grants for the improvement of state courts. Information on such grants and other aspects of state courts.

Tarr, G. Alan. *Understanding State Constitutions.* Princeton, N.J.: Princeton University Press, 1998. Informative book about the development and interpretation of state constitutions.

Robert A. Carp, Ronald Stidham, and Kenneth L. Manning, *The State Courts*, (Washington, DC: CQ Press, 2010).

3. JURISDICTION AND POLICYMAKING BOUNDARIES

In setting the jurisdictions of state courts, the constitutions and legislatures mandate the types of cases each court can hear. The role of legislative bodies in setting courts' jurisdiction is an ongoing one, and in this chapter we consider how lawmakers can influence judicial behavior by redefining the types of cases judges can hear. We also provide a detailed discussion of judicial self-restraint, examining ten principles, derived from legal tradition and constitutional and statutory law, that govern a judge's decision about whether to review a case. We begin, however, with a brief look at the jurisdiction of state courts and the two major categories of cases that define the overall workload of the state courts.

JURISDICTION OF STATE COURTS

The jurisdictions of the fifty separate state court systems in the United States are established in virtually the same manner. Each state has a constitution that sets forth the authority and decision-making powers of its trial and appellate judges. Likewise, each state legislature passes laws that spell out the specific powers and prerogatives of judges and the obligations of those who sue in the state courts. Because no two state constitutions or legislative bodies are alike, it is not surprising that the jurisdictions of state courts vary from one state to another. One state constitution may give its supreme court **original jurisdiction** over all cases in which a state is suing one of its counties, and another state constitution may confer such jurisdiction only on the low-level circuit courts. One state legislature might define felony theft as the stealing of $3,000 or more, sending the case automatically to a county criminal court, but a case involving less than $3,000 would go to a municipal court authorized to handle only minor crimes. In another state, the legislature might draw the line between felony and petty theft at $2,000. But, even though court jurisdictions vary from one state to another and from the national model, they are all derived in part from a constitution and in part from enactments of legislative bodies.

Criminal Cases

A criminal case commences when a local district attorney has reason to believe that a violation of the state penal code has occurred. After obtaining an **indictment** from a **grand jury** or proceeding with a **bill of information,** the district attorney's office files charges against the accused in the regional trial court of original jurisdiction authorized to hear such cases. Criminal activity, as defined by the state legislature, covers a wide range of behavior, including automobile theft, drug trafficking, burglary, assault, arson, rape, and murder.

After charges are filed against an accused, and if no **plea bargain** has been made, a formal trial will take place. In court the defendant has whatever rights he is given in the state constitution and those rights contained in the due process clause of the Fourteenth Amendment as interpreted by the U.S. Supreme Court. Among these rights is to be represented by counsel, at state expense, if the defendant is unable to pay for an attorney. Defendants may waive the right to a trial by a jury of their peers. A defendant who is found not guilty of the crime is set free and may never be tried again for the same offense (the Fifth Amendment's protection against double jeopardy). If the accused is found guilty, the judge determines the appropriate sentence within a range set by the state legislature, and the length of a sentence cannot be appealed so long as it is within the range prescribed by the legislature. The government may not appeal a verdict of not guilty, but convicted defendants may appeal to an intermediate appellate court or the court of last resort, according to the route(s) of appeal in that particular state, if they believe that the judge or jury made an improper legal determination.

Civil Cases

A majority of the state court caseload is civil in nature; that is, it consists of suits between private parties or between the state government, acting in its nonprosecutorial capacity, and a private party. Civil cases that originate in the state trial courts may be placed in several categories. The first is litigation concerning the interpretation or application of that state's constitution or acts of its legislature. Examples of cases in this category include the following: a petitioner claims that one of her state-protected civil rights has been violated or a litigant alleges that he is being harmed by an unconstitutional state statute. The point is that a state question must be raised for the state trial courts to have jurisdiction. It is not enough to say that the state courts should hear a case "because this is an important issue" or "because an awful lot of money is at stake." Unless one is able to invoke the state constitution or a state law, the case must be litigated elsewhere (probably in the federal courts).

Some minimal dollar amounts may apply in certain types of cases before a particular trial court may hear them. Recall from Chapter 1, for example, that local trial courts of limited jurisdiction may hear only civil disputes involving $3,000 or less, and suits for more than $3,000 are heard by state trial courts of general jurisdiction. Some types of cases, on the other hand, must be heard by the federal instead of the state judiciary. Civil rights cases, such as those covered by the Voting Rights Act of 1965, provide a good example.

JURISDICTION AND LEGISLATIVE POLITICS

One political reality regarding the jurisdiction of American courts that cannot be overemphasized is that for all intents and purposes, Congress and the fifty state legislatures determine the types of issues and cases the courts in their separate realms will hear. And equally important, what the omnipotent legislative branches give, they may also take away. Some judges and judicial scholars argue that the U.S. Constitution (in Article III) and the respective state documents confer a certain inherent jurisdiction on the judiciaries in some areas, independent of the legislative will. Nevertheless, the jurisdictional boundaries of American courts clearly are a product of legislative judgments—determinations often flavored with the bittersweet spice of politics.

The legislature may advance a particular cause by giving courts the authority to hear cases in a public policy realm that previously had been forbidden territory for the judiciary. Conversely, it may discourage a particular social movement by passing legislation to make it virtually impossible for its advocates to have any success in the courts.[1] When the Hawaii Supreme Court approved same-sex marriages in 1993, a conservative and frightened Congress was determined to discourage judges in other states from rendering similar decisions. The result was the Defense of Marriage Act, which President Bill Clinton signed into law on September 20, 1996. The law was designed in part to prevent judges—both state and federal—from reading any meaning into the Fourteenth Amendment to the U.S. Constitution that would condone same-sex marriages. Among other things, the law defined marriage as "only a legal union between one man and one woman," and it permitted state courts to ignore judgments from courts in other states "respecting" marriages between two persons of the same gender. Between the controversial Hawaii Supreme Court ruling in 1993 and 2006, some forty-five states passed legislation specifically to ban gay marriages.[2] By the summer of 2009 state support for gay marriage seemed to rebound, and same-sex marriages are now legal in Connecticut, Iowa, Massachusetts, New Hampshire, Vermont, and the District of Columbia. Furthermore, other states have debated the issue or adopted varying degrees of "same-sex partnership" recognition. In addition, twenty states and more than 180 cities and counties ban discrimination against gay and lesbian individuals.[3] In other words, while discussing what courts do or may do, we must not lose sight of the commanding reality that just as the jurisdiction of U.S. courts is established by "the United States of America in Congress assembled," the jurisdictions of courts in the states are very much governed by—and the political product of—the will of the state legislatures.

JUDICIAL SELF-RESTRAINT

The activities that judges are forbidden to engage in, or at least are discouraged from engaging in, deal not so much with technical matters of jurisdiction as with **justiciability**—the question of whether judges in the United States ought to hear or refrain from hearing certain types of disputes. It is only by exploring both sides of this issue that insight into the role and function of the federal and state courts can be gained. In the following sections, ten separate aspects of **judicial self-restraint,** ten principles that serve to check and contain the power of American judges, will be examined.[4] These maxims originate from a variety of sources—the U.S. Constitution and state constitutions, acts of Congress and of state legislatures, the common law tradition—and, whenever possible, their roots and the nature of their evolution will be noted. Some apply more to appellate courts than to trial courts, as will be indicated. Finally, although we may offer an example from either the federal or state judiciary, most apply to both federal and state judges alike.

A Controversy Must Exist

The federal and state constitutions contain language indicating that the judicial power extends to cases in law and equity arising under the Constitution and laws of the United States or the state. The key word here is cases. Historically, judges have chosen to interpret the term in its most literal sense; there must be a controversy between legitimate adversaries who have met all the technical legal standards to institute a suit. The dispute must concern the protection of a meaningful, nontrivial right or the prevention or redress of a wrong that directly affects the parties to the suit. Three corollaries to this general principle breathe a little life into its rather abstract-sounding admonitions.

The first is that the courts do not render **advisory opinions,** rulings about situations that are hypothetical or that have not caused an authentic clash between adversaries. A dispute must be real and current before a court will agree to accept it for adjudication. For example, in 1902 Congress passed a law allocating certain pieces of land to the Cherokee Indians. Because such disbursements often stimulate many questions about property rights, Congress sought to head off any possible disputes by authorizing certain land recipients to bring suits against the U.S. government in the court of claims, with appeal to the Supreme Court. They were permitted to do so "on their own behalf and on behalf of all other Cherokee citizens" who received land "to determine the validity of any acts of Congress passed since the said act." Stripped of the legalese, the law said: "If you have any hypothetical questions about how the law might affect anyone, just sue the United States, and the courts will answer these questions for you." The Supreme Court politely but pointedly said, "We don't do that sort of thing; we settle only real, actual cases or controversies." The act of Congress was found to be nothing more

> than an attempt to provide for judicial determination, final in this court, of the constitutional validity of an act of Congress. [It] is true the United States is made a defendant to this action, but *it has no interest adverse to the claimants.* The object is not to assert a property right as against the government, or to demand compensation for alleged wrongs because of action on its part.... In a legal sense the judgment [amounts] to no more than an expression of opinion upon the validity of the [1902 act]. If such actions as are here attempted [are] sustained, the result will be that this court, instead of keeping within the limits of judicial power, and deciding cases or controversies arising between opposing parties, [will] be required to give opinions in the nature of advice concerning legislative action—a function never conferred upon it by the Constitution.[5]

A second corollary of the general principle is that the parties to the suit must have proper **standing.** This requirement deals with who may bring litigation to court. Although the term *standing* has many aspects, the most prominent component is that the person bringing suit must have suffered (or be immediately about to suffer) a direct and significant injury. As a general rule, a litigant cannot bring a claim on behalf of others (except for parents of minor children or in a special type of suit called a **class action).** In addition, the alleged injury must be personalized and immediate—not part of a generalized **complaint.** The main point, again, is that no judicial rulings are made on the merits of a case unless and until someone is able to convince the court that she will suffer or has suffered real injury from the objectionable law.

The third corollary of this general principle is that courts ordinarily will not hear a case that has become **moot**—when the basic facts or the status of the parties has significantly changed in the interim between when the suit was filed and when it comes before the court. The death of a litigant or a settlement between the litigants would render a case moot in most tribunals.

In 1974 the U.S. Supreme Court agreed to hear a petition from Marco DeFunis, who challenged the constitutionality of the admissions policy of the University of Washington Law School. The law school gave preferential treatment to certain minority racial groups, even though such applicants did not rate as high as other, nonminority applicants according to the school's evaluation procedures based on objective tests and grades. DeFunis, a nonminority applicant, charged reverse discrimination in violation of his Fourteenth Amendment rights. During the initial trial of this case at the state court level, DeFunis had been admitted to the law school (on a sort of conditional basis), and when the case eventually reached the Supreme Court, he was in his final quarter of law school. (The law school conceded at **oral argument** before the Court that it would permit DeFunis to graduate if he continued to fulfill all requirements.) When the Court learned of this, a majority determined that the case had become moot. "The controversy between the parties has thus ceased to be 'definite and concrete' and no longer 'touches the legal relations of parties having adverse legal interests,' " according to the Court.[6]

Sometimes, however, judges for their own reasons may decide that a case is still ripe for adjudication, even though the status of the facts and parties would seem to have radically altered. Examples include cases where someone has challenged a state's refusal to permit an abortion or to permit the life-support system of a terminally ill person to be switched off. (In such cases, by the time the suit reaches an appellate court, the woman may already have given birth or the moribund person may have died.) In these cases the judges believed that the issues were so important that they needed to be addressed by the court. To declare such cases moot would, practically speaking, prevent them from ever being heard in time by an appellate body.

A great deal of flexibility and common sense is built into the U.S. legal system—factors that allow for discretion in judges' decision making. The principle of judicial self-restraint offers a counterpoint, guiding judges in what they may not do. They may not decide an issue unless there is an actual case or controversy. From this it follows that they do not consider abstract, hypothetical questions; they do not take a case unless the would-be litigants can demonstrate direct and substantial personal injury; and they (usually) do not take cases that have become moot. This principle is important because it means that judges are not free to wander about the countryside like medieval knights slaying all the evil dragons they encounter. They may rule only on concrete issues brought by truly injured parties directly affected by the facts of a case.

Although federal judges do not rule on abstract, hypothetical issues, "high courts in eleven states (and a number of countries) provide advisory opinions on pending legislation when requested by the executive or legislative branch of government."[7] Also, American judges are empowered to render **declaratory judgments,** which define the rights of various parties under a statute, will, or contract. The judgments do not entail any type of coercive relief. As Justice William Rehnquist once put it, "A declaratory judgment is simply a statement of rights, not a binding order."[8] Although a difference exists between an abstract dispute that judges must avoid and a situation where a declaratory judgment is in order, in the real world the line between the two is often a difficult one for jurists to draw.

A Plea Must Be Specific

Another constraint on the judiciary is that judges will hear no case on the merits unless the petitioner is first able to cite a specific part of the Constitution as the basis of the plea. For example, the First Amendment forbids government to make a law "respecting an establishment of religion," which means, among other things, that the government may not provide direct financial aid to religious entities. In an effort to improve some of its poorly rated public school systems, the state of Ohio enacted its Pilot Project Scholarship Program, which provides financial assistance to families in any Ohio school district that is or has been "under federal court order requiring supervision and operational management of the district by the state superintendent." (Cleveland became the only Ohio school district to fall within that category.) In the 1999–2000 school year, fifty-six private schools participated in the program, and of these, forty-six (or 82 percent) had a religious affiliation. Furthermore, of the 3,700 students who participated in the scholarship program, 96 percent enrolled in religiously affiliated schools. In 2002 this program was challenged in the Supreme Court by those who argued that this flow of government aid to schools with a religious affiliation violated the First Amendment's ban on governmental "establishment of religion." [9] Ultimately the Supreme Court, in a divided vote, disagreed with the petitioner, arguing that the aid to religion was indirect rather than direct, because the government money went primarily to the parents. But no one could deny that the original petitioners had relied on a specific portion of the Constitution (the establishment clause) as part of their plea.

If one went into court and contended that a particular law or official action "violated the spirit of the Bill of Rights" or "offended the values of the founders," a judge would dismiss the proceeding on the spot. If judges were free to give concrete, substantive meaning to vague generalities such as these, there would be little check on what they could do. Who is to say what is the "spirit of the Bill of Rights" or the collective motivation of those who hammered out the state's constitution? Judges who were free to roam too far from the specific clauses and strictures of the constitutional document itself would soon become judicial despots.

In the real world, however, this principle is not as simple and clear-cut as it sounds, because the Constitution contains many clauses that are open to a wide variety of interpretations. The Constitution forbids Congress to pass any law abridging "freedom of speech," but this term has been virtually impossible for jurists to define with any degree of precision. The Eighth Amendment prohibits "excessive bail" for criminal defendants, but what is excessive? The Fourteenth Amendment, section 1, forbids states to abridge "the privileges and immunities of citizens of the United States," but who is to say what these privileges and immunities are? The Constitution gives hardly a clue. Although petitioners must cite a particular constitutional clause as the basis for their plea—as opposed to some ambiguous concept—there are enough vague clauses in the Constitution to give American judges plenty of room to maneuver and make policy.

Beneficiaries May Not Sue

A third aspect of judicial self-restraint is that a case will be rejected out of hand if the petitioner has apparently been the beneficiary of a law or an official action that he has subsequently chosen to challenge. Suppose that Farmer Brown has long been a member of the Soil Bank Program (designed to cut back on grain surpluses). Under the program, he agreed to take part of his land out of production and periodically was paid a subsidy by the federal government. After years as a participant, he learns that his lazy, ne'er-do-well neighbors, the Joneses, are also drawing regular payments for letting their farmland lie fallow. The idea that his neighbors are getting something for nothing starts to offend Farmer Brown, and he begins to harbor grave doubts about the constitutionality of the whole program.

Armed with a host of reasons that Congress had acted illegally, Brown challenges the legality of the Soil Bank Act in the local federal district court. As soon as it is brought to the judge's attention that Farmer Brown had himself been a member of the program and had gained financially from it, the suit is dismissed. One may not benefit from a particular governmental endeavor or official action and subsequently attack it in court.

Appellate Courts Rule on Legal—Not Factual—Questions

In the real world, appellate court justices often find it difficult to tell whether a particular legal dispute is a question of who did what to whom (the facts of the case) or of how to weigh and assess a series of events (the legal interpretation of the facts). A working proposition of state and federal appellate court practice is that these courts will generally not hear cases if the grounds for appeal are that the trial judge or jury wrongly amassed and identified the basic factual elements of the case. It is not that trial judges and juries always do a perfect job of making factual determinations. Rather, they are believed to be closer, sensorially and temporally, to the parties and physical evidence of the case. The odds are, so the theory goes, that trial judges and juries will do a much better job of making factual assessments than would an appellate body reading only a stale transcript of the case some months or years after the trial.[10] Legal matters—which laws to apply to the facts of a case or how to assess the facts in light of the prevailing law—are appropriate for appellate review. On such issues collegial, or multi-judge, appellate bodies presumably have a legitimate and better capacity "to say what the law is," as Chief Justice John Marshall put it.

Nevertheless, some qualification must be offered. In most jurisdictions, appellate courts will hear appeals under "the clearly erroneous rule," that is, when the petitioner contends that the trial court's determination of the facts was obviously and utterly wrong. The issue would not be a minor quibble about what the facts were but a belief that the trial court had made a finding that totally flew in the face of common sense. Likewise, appellate courts may be willing to review an administrative agency's factual determinations that were allegedly made "without substantial evidence." Despite these qualifications, it is still fair to say that trial courts are the primary determiners of the facts or evidence in cases, even though such determinations are not always absolutely conclusive.

For example, if X were convicted of a crime, and the sole grounds for her appeal were that the judge and jury had mistakenly found her guilty (that is, incorrectly sifted and identified the facts), the appeals court would probably dismiss the case out of hand. Assume, however, that X provided evidence that she had asked for and been refused counsel during her police interrogation and that her confession was therefore illegal. At trial the judge ruled that the Fifth Amendment's right against self-incrimination did not apply to X's interrogation by the police. The defendant argued to the contrary. Such a contention could be appealed because the issue is one of legal, not factual, interpretation.

That U.S. appellate courts are generally restricted to interpreting the law and not to identifying and assembling facts is one additional check on the scope of their decision making.

The Court Is Not Bound (Technically) by Precedents

If the state or federal high court overturns or circumvents past and supposedly controlling precedents when it decides a case, is the court practicing **judicial activism?** The answer is no; rather, this practice must be placed in the restraint column. If the state supreme court were inescapably bound by the dictates of its prior rulings, it would have very little flexibility. It would not be free to back off when discretion advised a cautious approach to a problem; it would not have the liberty to withdraw from a confrontation that might prove detrimental to the state's or the court's interests. By occasionally allowing itself the freedom to overrule a past decision or to ignore a precedent that would seem to be controlling, the supreme court establishes a corner of safety to which it can retreat if need be. When wisdom dictates that the court change direction or at least keep an open mind, this principle of self-restraint is readily plucked from the judicial kit bag.

Other Remedies Must Be Exhausted

Another principle of self-restraint often frustrates the anxious litigant but is essential to the orderly administration of justice: courts in the United States will not accept a case until all other remedies, legal and administrative, have been exhausted. Although this caveat is often associated with the U.S. Supreme Court, it is a working principle for virtually all American judicial tribunals. In its simplest form this doctrine means that legal petitions must work their way up the ladder. Cases must first be heard by the trial courts, then reviewed by an appellate tribunal (if the state has an intermediate appellate court), and finally heard by the state's highest court. This orderly procedure must and will occur despite the importance of the case or of the petitioners who filed it.

Exhaustion of remedies refers to possible administrative relief as well as adherence to the principle of a two-or three-tiered judicial hierarchy. Such relief might be in the form of an appeal to an administrative officer, a hearing before a board or committee, or formal consideration of a matter by a legislative body. Consider a hypothetical illustration. Professor Benjamin Wheatley is denied tenure at a staunchly conservative institution. He is told that tenure was not granted because of his poor teaching record and lack of scholarly publications. He contends that denial of tenure is in retaliation for his having founded the nearby Sunshine Socialist Society, a nudist colony for gay atheists. He has the option of a hearing before the university's Grievance Committee, but he declines it, saying, "It would do no good; it would just be a waste of time." Instead, he takes his case immediately to the local trial court, claiming that his constitutional rights have been violated. When the case is brought before the trial court, the judge says to Professor Wheatley: "Before I will even look at this matter, you must first take your case before the official, duly established Grievance Committee at your university. It doesn't matter whether you believe that you will win or lose your petition before the committee. You must establish your record there and avail yourself of all the administrative appeals and remedies that your institution has provided. If you are then still dissatisfied with the outcome, you may at that time invoke the power of the state district courts."

Judicial restraint, therefore, means that judges do not jump immediately into every controversy that appears to be important or strikes their fancy. The restrained and orderly administration of justice requires that before any court may hear a case, all administrative and inferior legal remedies must first be exhausted.

Courts Do Not Decide "Political Questions"

U.S. judges are often called on to determine the winner of a contested election, to rule on the legality of a newly drawn electoral district, or to get involved in voting rights cases. How, then, can the argument be made that **political questions** are out of bounds for the American judiciary? The answer lies in the narrow, singular use of the word *political.* To U.S. judges, the executive and legislative branches of government are political in that they are elected by the people for the purpose of making public policy. The judiciary, in contrast, was not designed by the founders to be an instrument manifesting the popular will and is therefore not political. According to this line of reasoning, a political question is one that ought properly to be resolved by one of the other two branches of government (even though it may appear before the courts wrapped in judicial clothing). When judges determine that something is a political question and therefore not appropriate for judicial review, what they are saying in effect is this: "You litigants may have couched your plea in judicial terminology, but under our form of government, issues such as this ought properly to be decided at the ballot box, in the legislative halls, or in the chambers of the executive."

When the state of Oregon gave its citizens the right to vote on popular statewide referendums and initiatives around the end of the nineteenth century, Pacific States Telephone and Telegraph Company objected.[11] (The company feared that voters would bypass the more business-oriented legislature and pass laws restricting its rates and profits.) The company claimed that by permitting citizens to directly enact legislation, the state has "been reduced to a democracy," whereas Article IV, section 4, of the Constitution guarantees to each state "a Republican Form of Government"—a term that supposedly means that laws are to be made only by the elected representatives of the people, not by the citizens directly. Pacific States Telephone demanded that the Supreme Court take action. Opting for discretion rather than valor, the high court refused to rule on the merits of the case, declaring the issue to be a political question. The Court reasoned that because Article IV primarily prescribes the duties of Congress, it follows that the founders wanted Congress—not the courts—to oversee the forms of government in the several states. In other words, the Court was being asked to invade the decision-making domain of one of the other (political) branches of government. And this it refused to do.

In 2003 Americans witnessed a circus-like political scenario in the state of Texas that some wanted the courts to resolve, but the judges would have none of it. The Republican-dominated legislature attempted to redraw congressional boundaries in the state to give the GOP four to seven additional seats in the Texas delegation to the U.S. House of Representatives. The Democratic minority in the Texas Senate, unable to defeat the redistricting bill in a straight party-line vote, opted to physically leave the state, thereby depriving the Senate of a quorum and preventing the obnoxious bill from being adopted. During the regular session of the legislature the Democratic senators fled to Oklahoma, and when the governor called a special session of the legislature for redistricting purposes, the Democrats hightailed it to the protective confines of New Mexico, where the Texas Rangers were without jurisdiction. The Republican governor and GOP Senate members repeatedly attempted to have the Texas courts order the wayward Democratic senators back to their posts, but even the all-Republican state supreme court unanimously refused to enter the fray. Putting aside the judges' legalese, the courts said this dispute was basically a political matter to be settled within the framework of the political process and/or ultimately by the voters of Texas. The courts do not enter what Justice Felix Frankfurter called "the political thicket."

The Burden of Proof Is on the Petitioner

Another weighty principle of self-restraint is the general agreement among the nation's jurists that an individual who would challenge the constitutionality of a statute bears the burden of proof. This is just a different way of saying that laws and official deeds are all presumed to be legal unless and until proven otherwise by a preponderance of evidence. The question of who has the burden of proof is of keen interest to lawyers because it determines which side has the bigger job to perform in the courtroom and which party must assume the lion's share of the burden of convincing the court—or lose the case entirely. Therefore, if a party is attacking a particular statute, he would have to do more than demonstrate that it was "questionable" or "of doubtful constitutionality"; instead, he would have to persuade the court that the evidence against the law was clear-cut and overwhelming—not often an easy task. In giving the benefit of the doubt to a statute or an executive act, judges have yet another area in which to exercise restraint.

The only exception to this burden of proof principle is in the realm of civil rights and liberties. Some jurists who are strong civil libertarians have long contended that when government attempts to restrict basic human freedoms, the burden of proof should shift to the government. And in several specific areas of civil rights jurisprudence, that philosophy now prevails. The U.S. Supreme Court has ruled in a variety of cases that laws that treat persons differently on the basis of their race or gender are automatically subject to a higher level of scrutiny than other laws. This means that the burden of proof shifts to the government to demonstrate a compelling or overriding need for this differential treatment. For example, the government has long argued (successfully) that some major restrictions can be placed on women in the armed forces to prevent them from being assigned to full combat duty.

Laws Are Overturned on the Narrowest Grounds Only

Sometimes during a trial a judge clearly sees that the strictures of the constitution have been offended by a legislative or executive act. Even here, however, ample opportunity is available to proceed with caution. Judges have two common ways to exercise restraint even when they must reach for the blue pencil.

First, a judge may have the option of invalidating an official action on statutory rather than constitutional grounds. Statutory invalidation means that a judge overturns an official's action because the official acted beyond the authority delegated to her by the law. Such a ruling has the function of saving the law itself while nullifying the official's misdeed.

Suppose that Congress continues to authorize postal officials to seize all obscene nude photographs that are shipped through the mail. A photographer attempts to mail pictures taken at his art studio, but the pictures are seized by postal officials. The photographer protests that the statute violates his First Amendment rights, and the case is eventually taken to the federal courts. Assuming that the judges are generally sympathetic to the position of the photographer, they have two basic options. They may declare the statute to be in violation of the Constitution and therefore null and void, or they may select another stance that permits them to have it both ways. They may decide that the law itself passed constitutional muster, but that the postal official in question mistakenly decided that the nude photos were obscene. The statute is preserved and a direct confrontation between the courts and Congress is averted, but the courts are able to give the petitioner virtually everything he wants. This is an example of deciding a case on statutory grounds.

Second, judges may, if possible, invalidate only that portion of a law they find constitutionally defective instead of overturning the entire statute. In 1963 Congress passed the Higher Education Facilities Act, which provided construction grants for college buildings. Part of the law declared that for a twenty-year period, no part of the newly built structures could be used for "sectarian instruction, religious worship, or the programs of a divinity school." Because church-related universities as well as state-supported institutions benefited from the act, the entire law was challenged in court as being in violation of the establishment clause of the First Amendment. The Supreme Court determined that the basic thrust of the law did not violate the Constitution, but it did find the "twenty-year clause" to be objectionable. After all, the Court reasoned, most buildings last a good deal longer than two decades, and a building constructed at public expense could therefore house religious activities during most of its lifetime. Instead of striking down the entire act, however, the Court majority merely substituted the word *never* for the words *twenty years.*[12] The baby was not thrown out with the bath water, and judicial restraint was maintained.

No Rulings Are Made on the "Wisdom" of Legislation

This aspect of judicial self-restraint is probably the least understood by the public, the most often violated by the courts, and yet potentially the greatest harness on judicial activism. What this admonition means, if followed strictly, is that the only basis for declaring a law or an official action unconstitutional is that it violates the federal or state constitution on its face. Statutes do not offend the constitution merely because they are unfair, fiscally wasteful, or bad public policy. Official actions can be struck down only if they step across the boundaries clearly set forth by the founders. If taken truly to heart, this means that judges and justices are not free to invoke their own personal notions of right and wrong or of good and bad public policy when they examine the constitutionality of legislation.

A keen expression of this phenomenon of judicial self-restraint is found in Justice Potter Stewart's dissenting opinion in *Griswold v. Connecticut.* The Court majority had struck down the state's law that forbade the use of contraceptive devices or the dissemination of birth control information. Stewart said, in effect, that the law was bad, but that its weaknesses did not make it unconstitutional.

> Since 1897 Connecticut has had on its books a law which forbids the use of contraceptives by anyone. I think this is an uncommonly silly law. As a practical matter, the law is obviously unenforceable, except in the oblique context of the present case.... But we are not asked in this case to say whether we think this law is unwise, or even asinine. We are asked to hold that it violates the United States Constitution. And that I cannot do.[13]

Another spin-off of this principle is that a law may be passed that all agree is good and wise but is nevertheless unconstitutional; conversely, a statute may legalize the commission of an official deed that all know to be bad and dangerous but does not offend the Constitution. Permitting the police to dispose of known criminals without benefit of trial would probably save taxpayers a good deal of money and reduce the crime rate, but it would be a clear prima facie violation of the Constitution. A congressional tax on every sex act might be constitutionally permissible but would be a very unwise piece of legislation—not to mention difficult to enforce. When laws or official acts are at issue, the adjectives *good* and *constitutional* are no more synonymous than are *bad* and *unconstitutional.*

Although few legal scholars would disagree with what has just been said, virtually all would point out that the principle of not ruling on the "wisdom" of a law is difficult to follow in the real world and is often honored in the breach. This is so because constitutions, often rather brief documents, are silent on many areas of public life and contain a number of phrases and admonitions that are open to a variety of interpretations. For example, the right to a jury trial is typically guaranteed in criminal cases in state courts, but exactly how many jurors does it take to guarantee a fair trial? As human beings, judges have differed in the way they have responded to this question. The Constitution guarantees a person accused of a crime the right to a defense attorney. But does this right continue if one appeals a guilty verdict and, if so, for how many appeals? Strict constructionists and loose constructionists have responded differently to these queries.

Despite the inevitable intrusion of judges' personal values into their interpretation of many portions of the Constitution, virtually every jurist subscribes to the general principle that laws can be invalidated only if they offend the Constitution—not the personal preferences of the judges.

SUMMARY

In this chapter we have focused on what American courts are supposed to do and on what they must refrain from doing. They adjudicate cases that come within their lawful original or appellate jurisdiction. Trial courts hear criminal cases and civil suits in the first instance. Intermediate appellate courts exist in most of the states and, having no original jurisdiction, handle appeals from the trial courts. State courts of last resort necessarily differ from state to state depending on whether the state has intermediate appellate courts. In the states that do have such courts, the state court of last resort is typically given some discretion to focus on only the most important state policy questions it is asked to review. On the other hand, if a state has no intermediate appellate tribunal, the highest court must naturally spend a good deal of its time on routine appeals as well as important questions of public policy. Chapter 2 summarized the primary contours of state court organization, but in this chapter we emphasized the behavior of state judges. That is, we talked more about what they can and cannot do as well as what is and is not expected of them.

In the U.S. legal system, courts generally are not to adjudicate questions unless a real case or controversy is at stake, although many state courts may render advisory opinions. All pleas to the courts must be based on a specific portion of the state or federal constitution. Judges are obliged to dismiss suits in which a petitioner is challenging a law from which he has benefited. Federal and state appellate courts may rule only on matters of law—not on factual questions. Not being bound entirely by its precedents, the supreme courts are free to exercise flexibility and restraint if they wish to do so. All courts insist that litigants exhaust every legal and administrative remedy before a case will be decided. Courts in the United States are to eschew political questions and insist that the burden of proof rests on those who contend that a law or official action is unconstitutional. If judges must nullify an act of the legislature or the executive, they are to do so on the narrowest grounds possible. Finally, courts ought not rule on the wisdom or desirability of a law but are to strike down legislation only if it clearly violates the letter of the Constitution.

FURTHER THOUGHT AND DISCUSSION QUESTIONS

1. Have you ever read your own state's Bill of Rights? Chances are that it guarantees as many, and as significant, liberties as are found in the U.S. Constitution, and that its protections may be even more extensive than those found in the U.S. Constitution. What are the merits of state protections extending beyond the federal Bill of Rights?

2. What would happen if the legislature, because it did not like the decisions the state courts were handing down in a particular policy area, passed a law that removed the subject matter from the courts' jurisdiction? Would the action be constitutional?

3. Are "activist" state judges as out of control as some critics claim? Are judges limited enough in what they can do? Who or what establishes those boundaries, and should they be changed?

4. Would it be a good idea if the governor, the state legislature, and other government agencies could get the courts to rule on the constitutionality of proposed government actions before they were put in place? Wouldn't considerable time and trouble be saved if courts were allowed to nip unconstitutional acts in the bud before they did any harm?

Notes

1. For a recent empirical study of the interaction between congressional legislation and its interaction with Supreme Court agenda setting, see Anna Harvey and Barry Friedman, "Ducking Trouble: Congressionally Induced Selection Bias in the Supreme Court's Agenda," *Journal of Politics* 71 (2009): 574–592.
2. Bennett Roth, "Gay Marriage Amendment Falls Short Again in Senate," *Houston Chronicle,* June 8, 2006.
3. Jacqueline L. Salmon, "Faith Groups Increasingly Lose Gay Rights Fights," *Washington Post,* April 10, 2009, A4.
4. For our discussion of the many aspects of judicial self-restraint, we acknowledge our debt to Henry J. Abraham, on whose classic analysis of the subject we largely relied. See Abraham, *The Judicial Process,* 7th ed. (New York: Oxford University Press, 1998), chap. 9.
5. *Muskrat v. United States,* 219 U.S. 346 (1911) (emphasis added).

6. *DeFunis v. Odegaard,* 416 U.S. 317 (1974).

7. James R. Rogers and Georg Vanberg, "Judicial Advisory Opinions and Legislative Outcomes in Comparative Perspective," *American Journal of Political Science* 46 (2002): 379.

8. *Steffel v. Thompson,* 415 U.S. 452 (1974) at 482.

9. *Zelman v. Simmons-Harris,* 536 U.S. 639 (2002).

10. One innovation in this realm is worth noting. At the present time in a few federal and state courtrooms, appeals judges are able to view the videotapes of trials whose judgments are appealed to them. For an interesting discussion of this practice and conjecture about its future implications, see Junda Woo, "Videotapes Give Appeals Cases New Dimensions," *Wall Street Journal,* April 14, 1992.

11. *Pacific States Telephone & Telegraph v. Oregon,* 223 U.S. 118 (1912).

12. *Tilton v. Richardson,* 403 U.S. 672 (1971).

13. *Griswold v. Connecticut,* 381 U.S. 79 (1965).

SUGGESTED RESOURCES

Abraham, Henry J. *The Judicial Process,* 7th ed. New York: Oxford University Press, 1998. A traditional but classic discussion of the judicial process, especially Chapter 9, which focuses on judicial self-restraint.

Halpern, Stephen C., and Charles M. Lamb, eds. *Supreme Court Activism and Restraint.* Lexington, Mass.: Lexington Books, 1982. An excellent series of individual essays about the history and the pros and cons of judicial activism and restraint.

Murphy, Walter F., C. Herman Pritchett, Lee Epstein, and Jack Knight, eds. *Courts, Judges, and Politics: An Introduction to Judicial Process,* 6th ed. New York: McGraw-Hill, 2006. A rich and varied collection of some of the most important historical documents in the realm of judicial process and behavior.

National Center for State Courts. Available online at www.ncsconline.org/searchncsc.html. Basic information and statistics about the organization and caseloads of state courts.

Tarr, G. Alan. *Understanding State Constitutions.* Princeton, N.J.: Princeton University Press, 1998. An important discussion of state courts as affected by changes in their own constitutions and by the effect of the "new judicial federalism."

Robert A. Carp, Ronald Stidham, and Kenneth L. Manning, *The State Courts*, (Washington, DC: CQ Press, 2010).

4. JUDGES IN STATE COURTS

This chapter focuses on the state judges themselves—the black-robed decision makers whom most Americans still regard with such great reverence. As we focus on these jurists, we need to keep some questions in mind. What characteristics do these people have that distinguish them from the rest of the citizenry? What are the qualifications—both formal and informal—for appointment to the bench? How are the judges selected and who are the participants in the process? How are judges socialized into their judicial roles; that is, how do judges learn to be judges? How are judges disciplined, and when are they removed from the bench?

QUALIFICATIONS AND BACKGROUNDS OF STATE JUDGES

Although the selection process for state judges differs across the land, the individuals tapped for judicial service at the state level tend to share with their federal colleagues the distinction of being local people who made good.

There were approximately 30,000 state judges, magistrates, justices of the peace, and other quasi-judicial officers in the United States in 2007.[1] This number has increased by about 5 percent over the past ten years as the number of cases and disputes has risen with the growth of the population.

The formal requirements to serve as a judge vary from state to state. Most states do not require justices of the peace or magistrates to have law degrees, but such degrees are usually required for trial and appellate judges. In addition, states often require at least some amount of legal experience—usually in the form of years as a licensed attorney—before one can serve on the bench. States also generally impose U.S. citizenship and state residency requirements, and a number of states impose minimum age requirements and/or mandatory retirement ages.

Unlike several other countries, the United States has neither a career judiciary nor a specifically prescribed training program for would-be judges. In France, by contrast, all prospective judges are trained for more than two years and can become judges only after passing rigorous competitive examinations. Judicial training in Scandinavian countries is acquired during a practical internship after graduating from law school.[2] Although it is fairly common in the United States to fill a vacancy on a higher court by promoting or electing a judge from a lower court, some of the leading judges of the nation's highest courts have had limited or no prior judicial experience. The chief justice of the Massachusetts Supreme Judicial Court, Margaret H. Marshall, was nominated to that court in 1996 even though she had no prior judicial experience. Marshall could, however, boast of a distinguished education that included a law degree from Yale University, a successful career as a partner at two major Boston law firms, and service as vice president and general counsel at Harvard University. Many state judges in Massachusetts at the time had the on-the-bench experience that Marshall lacked, but, given her distinguished background and experience, there was no real question that Marshall was qualified for the position. Although the legal profession is aware of the advantages of a career judiciary, "[I]t is generally thought that they are outweighed by the experience and independence that lawyers bring to the bench." [3]

The informal qualifications for being a state jurist are reflected in the socioeconomic profile that seems to hold throughout the United States. As far as gender goes, it used to be that judging was exclusively a man's business. But this has begun to change. At one time a woman lawyer was rare; now approximately one-third of lawyers in the United States are women. The gender balance will certainly continue to change as almost half of all law students today are women. Despite the upsurge in recent decades in the number of women in the legal profession and the number appointed to the bench, however, women remain underrepresented in the judiciary. In 2009, the National Association of Women Judges reported that 26 percent of state trial court jurists were female, while 29 percent of jurists on state supreme courts were women.[4] This figure was up slightly from 2000 when women constituted around 26 percent of state supreme court justices.[5] Still, the advances made in recent decades are worth noting. Only ten women served on state courts of last resort during the years 1980–1981;[6] by 2009, that number had risen to 104.

In the same vein, nonwhites remain a distinct minority among judges. Recent data collected by the American Bar Association notes that 10.1 percent of judges on state courts are persons of color. Of these jurists, approximately 6 percent are African American, about 2.8 percent are Latino, around 1 percent are Asian American, and only .1% are Native American.[7] Although white judges predominate by approximately nine out of ten, the number of minority jurists has risen substantially since the early 1980s and mid-1990s.[8]

State judges were at one time very likely to be closely tied to their region, but this too has changed somewhat. A 2000 study found that only 65.7 percent of the occupants of state high courts at that time were born in the state in which they were serving, a decline of more than 12 percent in a twenty-year period.[9] In addition, fewer state supreme court justices are receiving their law degrees from in-state institutions than was the case in the past.[10]

As far as political party affiliation goes, the balance between Democrats and Republican judges rises and falls with the political tides. In Georgia, for example, Republicans have been on the rise since the 1990s as Democrats lost power in the state. Conversely, Democrats in New Hampshire have made major gains in a state that used to be a Republican Party stronghold. Nationwide, the data suggest a reasonable level of partisan balance. In 2000 a slight majority (51.8 percent) of state high court justices sitting were Democrats, compared with 64.3 percent in 1994. Of the remainder, 46.2 percent were affiliated with the Republican Party, and only 2 percent were independents or had no political party affiliation.[11] In Canada, by contrast, judges pride themselves on not being chosen on the basis of their politics. One author noted, after interviewing Canadian judges, that several judges went out of their way to note that they were appointed to the superior trial courts by one party and then elevated to the provincial court of appeal by another.[12]

Serving as a prosecutor was the career path chosen by about one-third of the justices serving on state courts of last resort in 2000.[13] Also, nearly 72 percent of those making it to their state's highest court had previous judicial experience.[14] Conversely, this means that about 28 percent of the justices began their judicial career on their state's highest court. As far as holding elected office before ascending to the bench goes, the most comprehensive study to date of the characteristics of judges on the state courts of last resort indicates that only 15 percent of those sitting were former elected officials.[15]

Selection Process for State Judges

At the state level various methods are used to select jurists, and each of them has many permutations. Basically, there are five routes to a judgeship in any one of the fifty states: partisan election, nonpartisan election, merit selection gubernatorial appointment, and appointment by the legislature. Tables 4–1 and 4–2 indicate which states use each of the methods for selecting judges for full terms in the trial courts of general jurisdiction and the courts of last resort.

TABLE **4-1** Methods of Selecting Judges for Full Terms in State Trial Courts of General Jurisdiction

Method	*State(s)*
Partisan election	Alabama, Illinois, Indiana, Kansas,[a] Louisiana, New Mexico,[b] New York, Pennsylvania, Tennessee, Texas, West Virginia
Nonpartisan election	Arkansas, California, Florida, Georgia, Idaho, Kentucky, Michigan, Minnesota, Mississippi, Montana, Nevada, North Carolina, North Dakota, Ohio, Oklahoma, Oregon, South Dakota, Washington, Wisconsin
Merit selection	Arizona,[c] Alaska, Colorado, Connecticut, Delaware, Hawaii, Iowa, Kansas,[a] Maryland, Massachusetts, Missouri, Montana, Nebraska, New Hampshire. Rhode Island, Utah, Vermont, Wyoming
Gubernatorial appointment	Maine, New Hampshire, New Jersey
Legislative appointment	South Carolina, Virginia

SOURCE: Data on judicial selection compiled by the American Judicature Society, found at www.judicialselection.us. NOTE: Some states use more than one method for various courts.

[a]Kansas allows for trial courts judges to be chosen through merit selection or partisan election, at the option of each judicial district.

[b]New Mexico has a hybrid system of judicial selection that includes merit selection, partisan elections, and retention elections. When a judicial vacancy occurs, the appropriate nominating commission recommends qualified candidates to the governor, and the governor makes an appointment. At the next general election, a contested partisan election is held to fill the seat for the remainder of the term. The successful candidate runs in retention elections thereafter. The threshold for retention is higher in New Mexico than in most other states; judges must receive at least 57 percent in affirmative votes to be retained.

[c]Arizona allows for merit selection from the most populated counties. Less populous counties may adopt merit selection with voter approval.

TABLE **4-2** Methods of Selecting Judges for Full Terms in State Courts of Last Resort

Method	*State(s)*
Partisan election	Alabama, Arkansas, Illinois, Louisiana, New Mexico,[a] Pennsylvania, Texas, West Virginia
Nonpartisan election	Georgia, Idaho, Kentucky, Louisiana, Michigan, Minnesota, Mississippi, Montana, Nevada, North Carolina, North Dakota, Ohio, Oregon, Washington, Wisconsin
Merit selection	Alaska, Arizona, California, Colorado, Connecticut, Delaware, Florida, Hawaii, Indiana, Iowa, Kansas, Maryland, Massachusetts, Missouri, Nebraska, New Hampshire, New York, Oklahoma, Rhode Island, South Dakota, Tennessee, Utah, Vermont, Wyoming
Gubernatorial appointment	Maine, New Jersey
Legislative appointment	South Carolina, Virginia

SOURCE: Data on judicial selection compiled by the American Judicature Society, found at www.judici.ilselection.ns.

[a]New Mexico has a hybrid system of judicial selection that includes merit selection, partisan elections, and retention elections. When a judicial vacancy occurs, the appropriate nominating com mission recommends qualified candidates to the governor, and the governor makes an appointment. At the next general election, a contested partisan election is held to till the seat for the remainder of the term. The successful candidate runs in retention elections thereafter. The threshold for retention is higher in New Mexico than in most other states; judges must receive at least 57 percent in affirmative votes to be retained.

But as is often the case in the political world, things are not always what they seem. In states that officially choose their judges for full terms by partisan elections, a good number of judges may receive their initial position through gubernatorial appointment. The appointment may come because a sitting judge has died or resigned or a new judicial position has been created, and the vacancy is then filled by the governor in accordance with state law. The newly appointed judge may eventually have to run for another term in a general election, but most incumbent judges are easily reelected. Likewise, in states that are officially in the nonpartisan election category—for example, Minnesota—it is often no secret which judicial candidate is the Democrat and which is the Republican, and the voters may respond accordingly.

Election of Judges

The election of judges, on either a partisan or a nonpartisan ballot, is a very common selection methodology among the states. Although almost unheard of in colonial days, this method became popular during the time of President Andrew Jackson—an era when Americans sought to democratize the political process.

In practice, things have not always worked this way. Before the 1980s, judicial elections "were traditionally uncompetitive, and the major causes of turnover on the bench were retirements and resignations." [16] Furthermore, uncontested races typically involved modest spending and low levels of candidate visibility. Very little information was imparted in judicial campaigns, and voters relied primarily on such cues as party affiliation and name familiarity.

This began to change in the late 1970s, and "the 1980s brought numerous examples of extremely competitive and remarkably expensive judicial elections." [17] The first signs of a new style of judicial elections appeared in California, where deputy district attorneys in Los Angeles advertised in a local legal newspaper to recruit candidates to run against sitting trial court judges. This campaign resulted in an unprecedented number of contested races and defeated incumbents. Subsequent judicial elections in California have been characterized by "preemptive fundraising and hiring political consultants early in the election season." [18] Naturally, these elections have also become quite a bit more expensive.

The amount of money spent on retention elections remains pretty low overall—a total of just over $1.5 million was spent in all the supreme court contests in the twenty states that had retention elections from 1999 to 2006.[19] Expenditures in contested state supreme court races, however, have exploded in recent years. In Texas supreme court candidates typically spent less than $200,000 before 1984.[20] In 2006 those vying for a seat on the high court in the Lone Star State spent just over $3.5 million, a 1,700 percent increase. A record was set in Illinois in 2004: the candidates raised more than $9.3 million in their bid to join the state's supreme court. But this record did not stand for long. In the 2005–2006 election cycle, Alabama state supreme court candidates raised a staggering $13,413,978, shattering the Illinois record by almost 50 percent.[21]

Indeed, in total state supreme court candidates in the United States raised almost $47 million for their races in 2004 and more than $33 million in 2006.[22] This trend toward increasing amounts of money in judicial elections is not limited to large or urban states, and all indications are that such increases will continue.

Another important change in judicial elections involves the source of campaign funds—a subject that raises concerns about the susceptibility of judges to accusations of favoritism. Judicial candidates raise campaign funds from a variety of sources: individuals (including lawyers with business before the court), political parties, and interest groups. In addition, some use their own money. One study found that about 40 percent comes from the judge's own personal funds, nearly 49 percent from individuals, 1.5 percent from political parties, and almost 5 percent from interest groups.[23]

The U.S. Supreme Court wrestled with this issue in 2009 in a case from West Virginia.[24] The Court ruled that excessive contributions to judges create an unconstitutional threat to a fair trial because they pose a risk of "actual bias" in cases involving their political benefactors.[25] The dispute centered on Don Blankenship, an executive for Massey Energy, a coal company. Blankenship spent $3 million in 2004 to help elect Brent Benjamin to the state Supreme Court, and once on the bench, Judge Benjamin voted to reverse a $50 million judgment against Massey Energy. Judge Benjamin declined calls to recuse himself from the case, even though the money that Blankenship spent was more than three times the total amount that all other Benjamin supporters gave.[26] In 2008 Elliot Maynard, another jurist on the West Virginia Supreme Court, lost his reelection bid after 2006 photos surfaced of Maynard vacationing with Blankenship on the posh French Riviera. A case involving Massey Energy was pending before the court at the time, and around a year after their European trip Judge Maynard cast the decisive vote in a multimillion dollar ruling that favored Massey Energy.[27]

The question of campaign contributions involves more that just wealthy business interests. Some suggest that lawyers make contributions to judicial candidates in the hope of receiving favorable treatment in the courts. In addition to seeing a friendly face on the other side of the bench, some lawyers may make a contribution in the hope that a judge will reward them with an appointment to provide some sort of compensated legal service.

On the other side of the coin, it is of some concern that lawyers may be asked to contribute to a judicial campaign. Lawyers with business before the court may find it difficult to refuse a solicitation for a contribution, especially if it comes from a sitting judge.

Interest-group giving to judicial campaigns also raises concerns, because some believe that the judiciary should be a nonpartisan branch of government. Judicial candidates, however, often see labor unions, business organizations, and other advocacy groups as important sources of funds.[28] Interest groups may be willing contributors because they view judicial elections as a way to influence court decisions by altering the composition of the bench.

Finally, we should note that the method of actually conducting a judicial campaign has changed over the years. Candidates, especially those running for an intermediate appellate court or a court of last resort, now place greater emphasis on broadcast television and less emphasis on traditional methods of contacting voters. In 2000 supreme court candidates in only one in four states with contested races advertised on television. By 2004 the percentage had jumped to four out of five.[29] In 2006 the voters in 91 percent of states with contested supreme court elections saw TV advertising.[30] Although many candidates for a judgeship still focus primarily on their qualifications and traits such as judicial temperament and fairness, others have begun to speak out more boldly on policy issues. In fact, the U.S. Supreme Court ruled in a 2002 case that the Minnesota Supreme Court's canon of judicial conduct, which prohibited a candidate for judicial office from announcing his or her views on disputed legal or political issues, violates the First Amendment's free speech clause.[31]

In summary, state judicial elections no longer simply subject judges to a cursory review by voters. As the authors of one study put it,

> now that electoral uncertainty forces candidates to raise money and gain the support of interested groups, they are subject to electoral pressures that are remarkably similar to those experienced by legislators, mayors, and other elected officials.[32]

As part of the Progressive movement at the turn of the twentieth century, reformers sought to take some of the raw partisanship out of judicial elections by having judges run on a nonpartisan basis. In principle they would run on their ideas and qualifications, not on the basis of which party they belonged to. In practice, however, a recent study reveals that candidates in nonpartisan elections also regard political parties and interest groups as important to their campaigns and as sources of campaign funds.[33]

Merit Selection

Undaunted, reformers have come up with a method other than nonpartisan elections to accomplish the goal of obtaining qualified state judges free from the taint of political bias. **Merit selection,** by whatever name, has been around since the early 1900s as a preferred method of selecting judges. The first state to fully adopt such a method was Missouri, in 1940, and such schemes have since become known as generic variants of "the Missouri Plan."

The states with Missouri-type plans use a combination of elections and appointments. In effect, this type of plan provides for much greater influence from lawyers than any other selection method. The governor appoints a judge from among several candidates recommended by a nominating panel of five or more people, usually including attorneys (often chosen by the local bar association), nonlawyers appointed by the governor, and sometimes senior judges. Either by law or by implicit agreement, the governor appoints someone from the recommended list. After serving for a short period of time, the newly appointed judge must stand for a retention election, at which time he or she, in effect, runs on his or her record. (The voters are asked, "Shall Judge X be retained in office?") If the judge's tenure is supported by the voters, as is virtually always the case, the judge will serve for a regular and fairly long term. Does a Missouri plan take politics out of the judicial selection process? After an exhaustive study of how the plan had operated in Missouri for more than a quarter century, two observers concluded that "it is naive to suggest ... that the Plan takes the 'politics' out of judicial selection." [34]

A highly publicized judicial retention contest in Tennessee shows what can happen when a judge is asked merely to run on her own record. Justice Penny White, who had been appointed to Tennessee's high court in 1994 after serving as a trial and court of criminal appeals judge, faced a retention election in August 1996 that became a referendum on the death penalty.[35] Justice White's most vocal opponents included the Tennessee Conservative Union, the Republican Party, and Republican governor Don Sundquist. The GOP mailed a brochure to voters that carried the slogan "Vote for Capital Punishment by Voting NO on August 1 for Supreme Court Justice Penny White." The brochure offered three cases as evidence that Justice White placed the rights of criminals before the rights of victims.

Supporters of Justice White mounted a counterattack based on the arguments that the entire court had reached the decisions and that Justice White did not write separate opinions in the cases.[36] The arguments in Justice White's behalf were to no avail, however, and she was removed from the bench.

The merit selection process still has plenty of room for politics. One student of retention elections notes that special interest groups have discovered that judicial retention elections "are vehicles by which offending judges can be unseated and state judicial policy making can be influenced." [37] The long-term picture, however, is not one of spectacular defeats but of judges being retained in large numbers. A study covering the years 1964 through 1998 found that "in only 52 of 4,588 judicial retention elections were judges not retained." [38]

Despite the unhappy anomalies that occasionally accompany this form of judicial selection and retention, it still has its supporters. Indeed, some surveys suggest that approximately 80 percent of the public supports the election of judges.[39] Nevertheless, because studies fail to document significant differences in the behavior of elected judges as compared with those selected under merit systems, support for merit selection may be more an act of faith than an argument based on well-documented findings.

Gubernatorial Appointment and Legislative Appointment

In the early days of the Republic, judges were chosen either by the governor or the state legislature, but today such methods are used in only a handful of states. When judges are appointed by the governor, politics almost invariably comes into play. In the dozens of appointment opportunities that arise, governors tend to select individuals who have been active in state politics and whose activity has benefited either the governor personally or the governor's political party or allies. Also, in making judicial appointments, the governor often bargains with local political bosses or with state legislators whose support is needed. A governor may also use a judgeship to reward a legislator or local politico who has given faithful political support in the past.

Only two states—Virginia and South Carolina—still allow their legislators to appoint state judges. Although a variety of criteria may be used in choosing members of the state supreme courts, when it comes to filling the state trial benches, state legislators often turn to former members of the legislature.[40] This does not mean that judges appointed in this way are merely political hacks in need of a job, but it is evidence that friends and colleagues do take care of their own when given the opportunity.

Judicial Selection Methods and the Recruitment of Women and Minorities

As noted earlier, state judiciaries are not particularly representative of the diversity of the country as a whole with respect to gender and ethnicity. We now examine whether one judicial selection method is more likely than another to enhance diversification of the bench. A study looking at representation of women and minorities on the state appellate courts in 1999 indicated that a slightly higher percentage of women and minorities attained their positions by judicial election (26.83 percent), as compared with being appointed in a merit selection system (24.86 percent). But an even higher percentage of women and minorities (28.18 percent) were appointed by the state's governor.[41] Similarly, a 2005 study found that almost 70 percent of minority judges in general jurisdiction courts obtained their position through partisan or nonpartisan elections.[42] The finding that women and minorities fare better in elections than in a merit plan would seem to indicate the importance of the U.S. Supreme Court's 1991 decision that the Voting Rights Act of 1965 fully applies to the election of state judges.[43] Another study, focusing specifically on gender diversity in state supreme courts, found that women are significantly more likely to reach the state supreme court by being appointed rather than by winning the judgeship in an election. Furthermore, when an appointment system is used, women are much more likely to be appointed to an otherwise all-male court.[44]

Most advocates of increased ethnic and gender diversity on the bench have argued that it is essential, at the very least, on the grounds of basic fairness to these groups. Others point to the symbolic importance of having the judiciary better reflect the gender and ethnic makeup of society as a whole. Whether the decision making of women and ethnic minority jurists (whom scholars sometimes call "nontraditional" judges) is—or should be—different from that of white males (that is, "traditional" judges) is still the subject of much debate. The results of numerous studies present a mixed picture, but in general the differences, if any, between traditional and nontraditional judges have tended to be modest, according to researchers.[45]

Judicial Selection: Debating Appointment versus Election

The question of which judicial selection method is better—appointment or election—is one that state political leaders, lawyers, interest groups, academics, and the public have long debated. As you might imagine, both sides have some powerful arguments in their favor, and both approaches present some problems and difficulties.

Supporters of judicial appointment argue that fundraising for these campaigns leads to serious questions about judicial independence. A process that requires both incumbent judges and those who aspire to sit on the bench to seek campaign contributions from lawyers and business interests is one that is ripe for corruption and improper influence of judges. It is a system that cause some to ask if justice is "for sale." [46] Furthermore, because judges do not render political judgments like legislators and governors do, some critics argue that it is inappropriate to select judges in the same manner as that of elected, political representatives.

Those who prefer judicial appointment plans also argue that electing judges on partisan ballots exposes judges to the ebb and flow of national party politics and presents the possibility of good, fair judges losing their position when their party is out of favor. Because the primary qualifications that are typically sought in judges—independence, ethical behavior, and fairness—are not dependent upon political party, it seems unwise to select judges based on party. Instead, supporters of judicial appointments argue that judges are better selected in a process that emphasizes qualifications and impartiality, a fair process that is not tainted by campaign contributions, electioneering, or political party popularity.

Another criticism of judicial elections concerns low voter participation rates. Because the United States has relatively low rates of voter turnout compared to most other world democracies, particularly in nonpresidential elections, some suggest that a lack of participation by the public mars the judicial election process. Is it really wise to have judges selected via elections in which only 30 percent or 35 percent of the electorate participates? Supporters of judicial appointments argue that a process that emphasizes the judicial candidate's background, experience, and judicial temperament would be more advantageous.

But the appointment process comes in for criticism, too. Supporters of judicial elections argue that the people—not political elites—should decide who their judges are.

An appointment system by definition vests the power to select judges in the hands of insiders, whether the governor, legislature, or a judicial board or commission. Supporters of judicial elections argue that in an appointment system it is inevitable that backroom deal making and cronyism come into play in terms of who gets nominated for positions on the bench. In this way, critics allege that the appointment system may sometimes place more emphasis upon *who* a judicial candidate knows rather than *what* he may know. These critics suggest that appointing judges is no less political than electing them. Those who prefer judicial elections also criticize the lifetime appointment systems that are found in some states because these systems do not provide the public with the direct opportunity to remove a bad judge from the bench.

Supporters of judicial elections can point to recent research suggesting that, at least when it comes to state supreme court elections, some of the criticisms regarding voter turnout leveled at judicial elections may be off base.[47] A 2009 study used sophisticated statistical techniques to dispute many of the arguments that critics have leveled at judicial elections. The scholars concluded that judicial elections are not without problems, but these problems may be found in *all* elections. In addition, they assert that just because courts are electorally independent does not guarantee that they will be impartial or prudent in their use of judicial power.[48]

Needless to say, this debate will probably never produce a clear consensus about the "right way" to select judges. It is also a debate that indirectly reveals one of the major advantages of a federal system. A one-size-fits-all policy of judicial selection throughout the United States would likely leave many state populations dissatisfied. Consider just three states: Massachusetts, Minnesota, and Mississippi. They are very different states with divergent political histories, cultures, and values. By leaving the state judicial selection process up to the states themselves, the U.S. political system allows for a variety of approaches to this issue.

THE RETIREMENT AND REMOVAL OF STATE JUDGES

Being burdened with judges too old and unfit to serve seems to be less a problem at the state level than at the federal level. A significant number of states have mandatory retirement provisions. The U.S. Supreme Court in 1991 ruled that such mandatory retirement plans do not violate federal law or the equal protection clause of the Fourteenth Amendment.[49] Minimum ages for retirement range from sixty-five to seventy-five, with seventy being the most common. Some states even go so far as to have declining retirement benefit plans for judges who serve beyond the desired tenure; that is, the longer they stay on the bench, the lower their retirement benefits. Observers say that such plans are often effective in getting old, workaholic jurists to start examining travel brochures.

Retirement plans, no matter how effective in getting the older judge to resign, are of little use against the younger jurist who is incompetent, corrupt, or unethical. Throughout American history the states have used procedures such as **impeachment,** recall elections, and concurrent resolutions of the legislature to rid themselves of the judge gone bad. In 2000 the New Hampshire House of Representatives impeached the state's supreme court chief justice, David Brock. The House alleged, among other things, that Brock lied under oath to impede an investigation of his court involving a fellow justice, Stephen Thayer. Thayer was accused of trying to influence the appointment of judges to hear an appeal in his own divorce case, and he resigned after the scandal became public in March 2000. Chief Justice Brock, however, was ultimately acquitted on all four counts brought against him. The evidence suggests that methods for judicial discipline and removal are only minimally effective, either because they prove to be politically difficult to put into operation or because of their time-consuming, cumbersome nature.

A number of states have set up special commissions, often made up of the judges themselves, to police their own members. Oklahoma's Court of the Judiciary heard an ethics complaint in 2004 brought against a state judge for "his repeated use of a device known as a penis pump during nonjury and jury trials in his courtroom and in the presence of court employees while serving in his capacity as a district judge." [50] The offending jurist was ultimately removed from the bench and convicted in 2006 of sex crimes.[51] More seriously, in 2009 Sharon Keller, the top judge on the Texas Court of Criminal Appeals, faced a disciplinary hearing before the Texas Commission on Judicial Conduct in a high-profile death penalty case. Lawyers for a condemned man, Michael Richard, called the court on the afternoon of September 25, 2007, to ask that the offices be kept open late to receive a last-minute appeal after the U.S. Supreme Court had issued an order earlier in the day in another death penalty case that provided grounds for delaying Richard's execution. (Requests for late filings due to late-breaking legal developments are routine in death penalty cases.) Keller refused to wait. "We close at 5," she told Richard's lawyers. The appeal was never filed, and Richard was executed a few hours later, even though the U.S. Supreme Court's ruling that day effectively put a nationwide halt to executions in the U.S. for months. In 2010, the Commission on Judicial Conduct officially reprimanded Keller for "willful or persistent misconduct" that "casts public discredit on the judiciary."[52] Judge Keller was not, however, removed from office.

These high-profile cases are somewhat exceptional, however, as reformers have given these types of commissions only fair-to-poor marks because the persons most familiar with the problem—the judges—are often loath to expose a colleague to public censure and discipline. One lawyer noted that of the jurists removed from their positions by the Texas Commission on Judicial Conduct, "virtually all were charged with multiple and repeated acts of misconduct." [53] Policing the state judiciaries remains a challenge that beckons champions of good government.

SUMMARY

This chapter began with a collective portrait of the men and women who have served in the state judiciaries. We noted that state jurists generally have had strong ties to the locales in which they have served and have come from a distinct stratum of American society. The result is a core of judges who share similar values and who therefore strive, with minimal coercion, to keep the judicial system functioning in a relatively harmonious manner. Although formal qualifications for a seat on the bench are few, tradition has established several informal criteria, including a reasonable degree of professional competence, the "right" political affiliation and contacts, at least some desire for the job, and a bit of luck thrown in for good measure.

Politics and the judiciary go hand in glove. If the governor appoints the judges, similarity of the values of the governor and the judicial nominees is the norm. If judges are elected—even on nonpartisan ballots—the political and judicial processes are still inexorably intertwined. Judicial decisions by state judges reflect both the process by which the judges are chosen and the values of those who choose them.

Retention elections, such as the one involving Justice Penny White in Tennessee, frequently reflect struggles between politically diverse groups in the state. As one student of the courts puts it, "Judicial retention elections thus become another access point by which special interest groups can influence policy making."

We also discussed the effects of different selection processes on ethnic and gender diversity on the bench. Although both categories have been increasingly represented in recent years, using all methods of selection, recent studies suggest that women are most likely to serve as a judge when the appointment method is used.

The differing approaches to selecting judges—appointment or elections—have their advantages and disadvantages. As is often the case in politics, there is probably no clear or perfect answer as to which is better. But, by leaving the question of state judicial selection up to the states themselves, the U.S. system allows for the representation of the public wishes at the state level and avoids a one-size-fits-all approach that would like leave many states dissatisfied.

The disciplining and removal of corrupt or mentally unfit judges remain a problem. Implementation of mandatory retirement plans and the establishment of peer policing commissions illustrate the states' commitment to addressing this problem.

FURTHER THOUGHT AND DISCUSSION QUESTIONS

1. How successful have states been in their efforts to remove politics from the judicial selection process? To what extent is it desirable, or even possible, to make judicial selection apolitical?

2. Should steps be taken to ensure that state judiciaries are representative of the general population in terms of gender and ethnicity? Why?

3. Are citizens well enough informed to evaluate judges' performances in retention elections or should such decisions be left to attentive experts?

Notes

1. Richard Schauffler, Robert LaFountain, Neal Kauder, and Shauna Strickland, *Examining the Work of State Courts, 2004: A National Perspective from the Court Statistics Project* (Williamsburg, Va.: National Center for State Courts, 2005), 16.
2. See Steven Vago, *Law and Society,* 6th ed. (Upper Saddle River, N.J.: Prentice Hall, 2000), 372.
3. Ibid., 373.
4. Statistics compiled by the National Association of Women Judges, www.nawj.org/us_state_court_statistics_2009.asp.
5. Chris W. Bonneau, "The Composition of State Supreme Courts, 2000," *Judicature* 85 (July-August 2001): 28.
6. Ibid.
7. American Bar Association, National Database on Judicial Diversity in State Courts, 2009, www.abanet.org/judind/diversity/national.html.
8. Bonneau, "The Composition of State Supreme Courts, 2000," 28–29.
9. Ibid.
10. Ibid.
11. Ibid.
12. Mark C. Miller, "Judicial Activism in Canada and the United States," *Judicature* 81 (1998): 264.
13. Bonneau, "The Composition of State Supreme Courts," 29.
14. Ibid.
15. Ibid.
16. Owen G. Abbe and Paul S. Herrnson, "How Judicial Election Campaigns Have Changed," *Judicature* 85 (May-June 2002): 287.
17. Roy Schotland, "Elective Judge's Campaign Financing: Are State Judges' Robes the Emperor's Clothes of American Democracy?" *Journal of Law and Policy* 57 (1985): 2.
18. Abbe and Herrnson, "How Judicial Election Campaigns Have Changed," 287.
19. James Sample, Lauren Jones, and Rachel Weiss, *The New Politics of Judicial Elections 2006.* Report by the Justice at Stake Campaign, http://brennan.3cdn.net/49c18b6cb18960b2f9_z6m62gwji.pdf.
20. See Kyle Cheek and Anthony Champagne, "Money in Texas Supreme Court Elections: 1980–1998," *Judicature* 84 (July–August 2000): 20–25.
21. Sample et al., *The New Politics of Judicial Elections 2006.*

22. See Deborah Goldberg, Sarah Samis, Edwin Bender, and Rachel Weiss, *The New Politics of Judicial Elections 2004: Report on State Supreme Court Elections* (Justice at Stake Campaign, 2004), 13–15; and Sample et al., *The New Politics of Judicial Elections 2006*, 60.
23. Abbe and Herrnson, "How Judicial Election Campaigns Have Changed," 289–290.
24. *Caperton v. Massey Coal*, 556 U.S. ____ (2009).
25. Adam Liptak, "Justices Tell Judges Not to Rule on Major Backers," *New York Times*, June 8, 2009, www.nytimes.com/2009/06/09/us/politics/09scotus.html.
26. Editorial, *Birmingham News*, June 14, 2009, http://blog.al.com/birmingham-news-commentary/2009/06/our_view_too_bad_the_us_suprem.html.
27. Ian Urbina. "West Virginia's Top Judge Loses His Re-election Bid." *New York Times*, May 15, 2008, www.nytimes.com/2008/05/15/us/15judge.html.
28. Abbe and Herrnson, "How Judicial Election Campaigns Have Changed," 294–295.
29. Goldberg et al., *The New Politics of Judicial Elections 2004*, 3.
30. Sample et al., *The New Politics of Judicial Elections 2006*, 2.
31. *Republican Party of Minnesota v. White*, 536 U.S. 765 (2002).
32. Abbe and Herrnson, "How Judicial Election Campaigns Have Changed," 295.
33. Ibid., 289, 294.
34. Richard A. Watson and Rondal G. Downing, *The Politics of the Bench and the Bar* (New York: Wiley, 1969), 331.
35. Our account of Justice Penny White's retention election is drawn from Stephen B. Bright, "Political Attacks on the Judiciary," *Judicature* 80 (1997): 165–173; and Traciel V. Reid, "The Politicization of Retention Elections: Lessons from the Defeat of Justices Lanphier and White," *Judicature* 83 (1999): 68–77.
36. Reid, "The Politicization of Retention Elections," 72.
37. Ibid., 77.
38. Larry Aspin, "Trends in Judicial Retention Elections, 1964–1998," *Judicature* 83 (1999): 79.
39. Robert Rackleff, "Judicial Elections: Still Fair and Balanced?" *Carnegie Reporter* 3, no. 4 (Spring 2006), 12–21.
40. Herbert Jacob, "The Effect of Institutional Differences in the Recruitment Process: The Case of State Judges," *Journal of Public Law* 13 (1964): 104–119; Bradley C. Canon, "The Impact of Formal Selection Process on the Characteristics of Judges—Reconsidered," *Law and Society Review* 6 (1972): 575–593; and Henry R. Glick and Craig F. Emmert, "Selection Systems and Judicial Characteristics," *Judicature* 70 (1987): 228–235.
41. See Mark S. Hurwitz and Drew Noble Lanier, "Women and Minorities on State and Federal Appellate Benches, 1985 and 1989," *Judicature* 85 (September-October 2001): 89.
42. American Bar Association, National Database on Judicial Diversity in State Courts, February 8, 2005. See www.abanet.org/judind/diversity/national.html#3.
43. See *Chisom v. Roemer*, 499 U.S. 380 (1991); *Houston Lawyers' Association v. Texas Attorney General*, 501 U.S. (1991).
44. Kathleen A. Bratton and Rorie L. Spill, "Existing Diversity and Judicial Selection: The Role of the Appointment Method in Establishing Gender Diversity in State Supreme Courts," *Social Science Quarterly* 83 (June 2002): 504.
45. See Cassia Spohn, "The Sentencing Decisions of Black and White Judges: Expected and Unexpected Similarities," *Law and Society Review* 24 (1990): 1197–1216; and David W. Allen and Diane E. Wall, "The Behavior of Women State Supreme Court Justices: Are They Tokens or Outsiders?" *Justice System Journal* 12 (1987): 232–245.
46. The CBS News program *60 Minutes* ran a segment on judicial corruption in Texas.
47. See Chris W. Bonneau and Melinda Gann Hall, *In Defense of Judicial Elections* (New York: Routledge, 2009).

48. Ibid, 138.
49. *Gregory v. Ashcroft*, 501 U.S. 452 (1991).
50. "Oklahoma Judge Accused of Using Sexual Device in Court," USA Today.com, June 25, 2004, www.usatoday.com/news/nation/2004-06-25-judge-conduct_x.htm.
51. "Okla. Ex-Judge Convicted in Penis Pump Case," Washingtonpost.com, June 30, 2006, www.washingtonpost.com/wpdyn/content/article/2006/06/30/AR2006063000416.html.
52. "Texas Judge Reprimanded in Death Row Case." New York Times, July 16, 2010. http://www.nytimes.com/2010/07/17/us/17judge.html.
53. Dan Boyd, "Sharon Keller Deserves Censure or Reprimand," *Dallas Morning News*, August 26, 2009, www.dallasnews.com/sharedcontent/dws/dn/opinion/viewpoints/stories/DN-boyd_27edi.State.Edition1.281e78b.html.

SUGGESTED RESOURCES

Abbe, Owen G., and Paul S. Herrnson. "How Judicial Election Campaigns Have Changed." *Judicature* 85 (May-June 2002): 286–295. An important study of all aspects of judicial elections in the states.

Baum, Lawrence. "Electing Judges." In *Contemplating Courts*, ed. Lee Epstein. Washington, D.C.: CQ Press, 1995, 18–43. Addresses the question of how voters choose between candidates for Ohio Supreme Court judgeships.

Bonneau, Chris W. "The Composition of State Supreme Courts, 2000." *Judicature* 85 (July-August 2001): 26–31. A useful study of the background characteristics of judges of state supreme courts.

Bonneau, Chris W., and Melinda Gann Hall. *In Defense of Judicial Elections*. New York: Routledge, 2009. A statistically sophisticated response to the criticism of judicial elections.

National Center for State Courts. Available online at www.ncsconline.org. An excellent source of research and information on state courts.

Sheldon, Charles H., and Nicholas P. Lovrich Jr. "State Judicial Recruitment." In *The American Courts: A Critical Assessment*, ed. John B. Gates and Charles A. Johnson. Washington, D.C.: CQ Press, 1991, 161–188. A good general review of the major selection methods for judges in the states and their advantages and disadvantages.

Stumpf, Harry P., and John Culver. *The Politics of State Courts*. New York: Longman, 1991. A general overview of state courts in the United States.

Robert A. Carp, Ronald Stidham, and Kenneth L. Manning, *The State Courts,* (Washington, DC: CQ Press, 2010).

5. LAWYERS, LITIGANTS, AND INTEREST GROUPS IN THE STATE COURTS

In this chapter we focus on three important actors in the judicial process: lawyers, litigants, and interest groups. Judges in the United States make decisions only in the context of cases brought to the courts by individuals or groups who have some sort of disagreement or dispute with each other. These adversaries, commonly called litigants, sometimes argue their own cases in minor forums such as small-claims courts, but they are almost always represented by lawyers in the more important judicial arenas.

LAWYERS

Because this book focuses on the work of state courts, it seems appropriate to look more extensively at the lawyers who handle cases in these courts. In some instances the litigants are private individuals and are represented by attorneys who are engaged in private practice. In other cases one of the parties involved in the suit may be the state. When that occurs, a government attorney as well as a private lawyer may participate in the case.

Government Attorneys in the Judicial Process

Government attorneys work at all levels of the judicial process, from trial courts to the highest state appellate courts. The bulk of the cases, however, never move beyond the trial courts.

Prosecutors at the State Level.

Those who prosecute persons accused of violating state criminal statutes are commonly known as district attorneys. In most states they are elected county officials, but in a few states they are appointed. The district attorney's office usually employs a number of assistants who do the bulk of the trial work. Most of these assistant district attorneys are recent graduates of law school and are using the position to gain trial experience. Many will later enter private practice, often as criminal defense attorneys. Others will seek to become district attorneys or perhaps judges after a few years.

The district attorney's office has a great deal of discretion in the handling of cases. Given budget and personnel constraints, not all cases can be afforded the same amount of time and attention. Therefore, some cases are dismissed, others are not prosecuted, and still others are prosecuted vigorously in court. Most cases, however, are subject to plea bargaining, which means that the district attorney's office agrees to accept the defendant's plea of guilty on a reduced charge or to drop some charges against the defendant in exchange for pleas of guilty on others.

District attorneys' offices are organized in different ways. Some use what is known as the horizontal, or zone, model. This model, often found in heavily populated areas, assigns assistants to different steps in the judicial process. Some screen cases that enter the prosecutor's office. Others are assigned to courts to deal with bond hearings, probable-cause hearings, misdemeanor cases, or felony cases. Still others specialize in presenting cases to the grand jury. Those assigned to a particular courtroom become part of the **courtroom work group,** with whom they interact more than they do with the assistant prosecutors who have other assignments.[1]

A second organizational model, found frequently in smaller jurisdictions, is the vertical prosecution model, which gives each assistant full responsibility for an assigned caseload. This means that one person receives the case when it is filed and follows it through to a final disposition.

Finally, some jurisdictions use a mixed model, which attempts to combine the best features of the other two models. Routine cases are likely to be handled in a horizontal model, and certain types of cases call for the vertical model. The district attorney's office may establish bureaus to deal with organized crime, repeat offenders, drug trafficking, or other special problems. Such bureaus are staffed with persons having special training or experience in the particular areas.

Public Defenders.

Often the person charged with violating a state criminal statute is unable to pay for the services of a defense attorney. In some areas a government official known as a public defender bears the responsibility for representing indigent defendants. The public defender therefore is a counterpart of the prosecutor. Unlike the district attorney, however, the public defender is usually appointed rather than elected.

Some parts of the country have statewide public defender systems; in other regions the public defender is a local official, usually associated with a county government. In New York City an independent organization known as the Legal Aid Society represents all indigent criminal defendants except those charged with murder.[2] New York's Legal Aid Society also has a civil division.

Like the district attorney, the public defender employs assistants and investigative personnel. The organizational scheme used by public defenders is similar to that of the prosecutor's office: horizontal, vertical or mixed.

State Attorneys General.

Each state has an attorney general who serves as its chief legal official. In most states this official is elected on a partisan statewide ballot.

The attorney general oversees a staff of attorneys who primarily handle civil cases involving the state. Although the prosecution of criminal defendants is generally handled by the local district attorneys, the attorney general's office often participates in investigating statewide criminal activities. Therefore the attorney general and his staff may work closely with the local district attorney in preparing a case against a particular defendant.

The state attorney general does not usually control appeals in the state courts, as the U.S. solicitor general does in the federal courts. Furthermore, the state attorney general normally argues cases before the state supreme court only when a state agency is involved in the case.

The state attorneys general also perform the important function of issuing advisory opinions to state and local agencies, which usually do not have their own legal staff. The attorney general's opinion will often interpret an aspect of state law not yet ruled on by the courts. Although the advisory opinion might eventually be overruled in a case brought before the courts, the attorney general's opinion may influence the behavior of state and local agencies.

Although state attorneys general are often seen simply as bureaucrats or managers of a state's Department of Justice, Mississippi attorney general Michael Moore has shown that they can also be innovative legal strategists. Moore became quite well known for the lawsuit he fashioned in 1994 against the tobacco industry. He focused on the cost to the state of treating smoking-related illnesses. Within a year, similar suits were filed by Florida, Minnesota, and West Virginia. By the end of 1998, forty-one state attorneys general had filed individual lawsuits against the tobacco industry. In the resulting settlement, the tobacco companies agreed to distribute $206 billion over twenty-five years to forty-six states, five commonwealths and territories, and the District of Columbia.[3]

Private Lawyers in the Judicial Process

In criminal cases in the United States the defendant has a constitutional right to be represented by an attorney. Some jurisdictions have established public defender's offices to represent indigent defendants. Others have devised a method of assigning a private attorney to represent a defendant who cannot afford to hire one. Those defendants who can afford to hire their own lawyers will do so.

Assigned Defense Counsel.

In many jurisdictions throughout the country, especially rural areas, the standard procedure is to appoint a private lawyer to represent an indigent defendant. Usually the assignment is made by an individual judge on an ad hoc basis. Local bar associations or lawyers themselves often provide the courts with a list of attorneys who are willing to provide such services. Compensation for representing an indigent defendant is generally based on a flat rate for hours spent in and out of court. The fee varies from area to area and often according to the case's complexity. It is usually a good deal less than an attorney would earn for providing services to a private client.

Private Defense Counsel.

Some attorneys in private practice specialize in criminal defense work. Such lawyers are more often found in solo practices or in small rather than large law firms. Although the private lives of criminal defense attorneys are depicted as glamorous on television, the average real-life criminal defense lawyer works long hours for low pay and low prestige.[4]

One of the major worries of the criminal defense attorney is getting paid. Because the clients are usually poor and often not trustworthy, the criminal defense lawyer generally requires advance payment of part of the fee. Often this is all the lawyer will collect. The average criminal defense attorney must therefore handle a large number of cases in order to survive. This heavy caseload means that the attorney must spend a great deal of time in court and in the office juggling cases. All told, the lawyer who specializes in criminal defense work typically leads a hectic life.

Legal Services for the Poor

Although criminal defendants are constitutionally entitled to be represented by a lawyer, defendants in a civil case or who wish to initiate a civil case do not have the right to representation. Those who cannot afford to hire a lawyer may find it difficult to obtain justice.

To deal with this problem, legal aid services of one sort or another are now found in many areas. Legal aid societies were established in New York and

Chicago as early as the late 1880s, and many other major cities followed suit in the twentieth century. Although some legal aid societies are sponsored by bar associations, most are supported by private contributions. Legal aid bureaus also are associated with charitable organizations in some areas. In addition, many law schools operate legal aid clinics to provide assistance for the poor as well as valuable training for law students.

Another source of legal help for indigents deserves mention. Many lawyers provide legal services **pro bono publico** (for the public good) because they consider this free assistance a professional obligation.

What about people who are not indigent but are too poor to hire a competent private attorney? Two relatively low-cost methods are available: legal clinics and prepaid legal plans.[5]

A legal clinic is a high-volume, high-efficiency law firm. These clinics depend on advertising and publicity to generate clients and keep costs down by relying on standard forms and delegating most of the routine work to paralegals. The clinics concentrate on fairly common legal problems such as divorces, traffic offenses, personal bankruptcies, and wills.

Prepaid legal plans, also referred to as legal insurance plans, may be financed in two ways. One method is to enroll a group of people, such as a labor union. Another method is to sign up individuals. Some plans make available a designated lawyer or group of lawyers from whom the client may choose. Other plans allow the client to choose any lawyer but usually place a limit on how much of the attorney's fee will be covered.

LITIGANTS

In some cases taken before the courts, the litigants are individuals, whereas in other cases one or more of the litigants may be a government agency, corporation, union, interest group, or university. In short, almost any individual or group has the potential to become a litigant in the courts.

What motivates a person or group to take a grievance to court? In criminal cases the answer to this question is relatively simple. A state or federal criminal statute has allegedly been violated, and the government prosecutes the party charged with violating the statute. In civil cases the answer is not so easy. Although some people readily take their grievances to court, many others avoid this route because of the time and expense involved. Still, enough cases are filed annually to cause concern about how the state courts can manage their dockets.

Political scientist Phillip Cooper points out that judges are called on to resolve two kinds of disputes: private law cases and public law controversies. Private law disputes are those in which one private citizen or organization sues another. Public law controversies involve the government more directly. In these situations a citizen or organization contends that a government agency or official has violated a right established by a constitution or statute. Cooper states that "legal actions, whether public law or private law contests, may either be policy oriented or compensatory."[6]

A classic example of private, or ordinary, compensation-oriented litigation is a suit brought by a person injured in an automobile accident against the driver of the other car in an effort to win monetary damages to compensate for the medical bills resulting from the accident. This type of litigation is personal and is not aimed at changing government or business policies.

Some private law cases, however, are policy-oriented or political in nature. Personal injury suits and product liability suits may appear, on the surface, to be simply compensatory in nature but may also be used to change the manufacturing or business practices of the private firms being sued.

A case litigated by former U.S. senator and one-time vice presidential candidate John Edwards of North Carolina, when he was a practicing lawyer in that state, provides a good example. The case began in 1993 after a five-year-old Raleigh, North Carolina, girl got stuck on the drain of a wading pool after another child had removed the drain cover. Such a powerful suction was created that, before she could be rescued, the drain had sucked out most of her large and small intestines. As a result, the girl will have to spend about eleven hours per day attached to intravenous feeding tubes for the rest of her life. In 1997 a jury awarded the girl's family $25 million in compensatory damages and, before the jury was to have considered punitive damages, the drain manufacturer and two other defendants settled for $30.9 million. Edwards said that the lawsuit revealed similar incidents in other areas of the country and presented a stark example of something industry insiders knew but others did not. Not only did the family win its lawsuit, but also the North Carolina legislature passed a law requiring multiple drains, which would be less powerful, to prevent such injuries in the future.[7]

Most political or policy-oriented lawsuits are public law controversies. That is, they are suits brought against the government primarily to stop allegedly illegal policies or practices. They may also seek damages or some other specific form of relief. A case decided in 1992 by the U.S. Supreme Court, *Lucas v. South Carolina Coastal Council,* provides a good example.[8] South Carolina's Beachfront Management Act forbade David H. Lucas to build single-family houses on two beachfront lots he owned. A South Carolina trial court ruled that Lucas was entitled to be compensated for his loss. The South Carolina Supreme Court reversed the trial court decision, and Lucas appealed to the U.S. Supreme Court. The high court ruled in Lucas's favor, saying that if a property owner is denied all economically viable use of his or her property, a taking has occurred and the Constitution requires compensation.

Political or policy-oriented litigation is more prevalent in the appellate courts than in the trial courts and is most common in the U.S. Supreme Court. Ordinary compensatory litigation is often terminated early in the judicial process because the litigants find it more profitable to settle their dispute or accept the verdict of a trial court. Litigants in political cases, however, generally do little to advance their policy goals by gaining victories at the lower levels of the judiciary. Instead, they prefer the more widespread publicity that is attached to a decision by an appellate tribunal. Pursuing cases in the appellate courts is expensive. Therefore, many lawsuits that reach this level are supported in one way or another by interest groups.

INTEREST GROUPS

Although interest groups are probably better known for their attempts to influence legislative and executive branch decisions, they also pursue their policy goals in the courts. Some groups have found the judicial branch to be far more receptive to their efforts than either of the other two branches of government. Interest groups lacking the economic resources to mount an intensive lobbying effort in Congress or a state legislature may find it much easier to hire a lawyer and locate a constitutional or statutory provision on which to base a court case. Likewise, a small group with few registered voters among its members may lack the political clout to exert much influence on legislators and executive branch officials. Large memberships and political clout are not prerequisites for filing suits in the courts, however.

Interest groups may also turn to the courts because they find the judicial branch more sympathetic to their policy goals than the other two branches. The National Association for the Advancement of Colored People (NAACP) provides an excellent example. This group, which dates from the early twentieth century, soon realized that legislative and executive branches generally were not sympathetic to the struggle for civil rights of black citizens. Seeing the courts as potentially more sympathetic, the NAACP started to focus its efforts on litigation as a means of achieving its goals. As the Supreme Court became more favorable to civil rights after 1937, the NAACP began to realize the value of the judiciary as a forum for its activities and eventually established the Legal Defense and Educational Fund, a separate organization composed of lawyers who represented them in litigation.

Following the pattern established by the NAACP, other minority group organizations began to use the courts. Cases dealing with the rights of Hispanics and women have been pursued vigorously by groups such as the Mexican-American Legal Defense and Education Fund and the National Organization for Women.

Throughout the 1960s interest groups with liberal policy goals fared especially well in the federal courts. In addition, the concept of the public interest law firm, attributed to consumer advocate Ralph Nader, gained prominence during this period. These law firms pursue cases that serve the public interest in general—including cases in the areas of consumer rights, employment discrimination, occupational safety, civil liberties, and environmental concerns.

In the 1970s, with the increasing conservatism of the federal courts stemming from President Richard Nixon's appointments, some major changes began to take place in the interaction between interest groups and the judiciary. Resuming the trend of the late nineteenth and early twentieth centuries, conservative interest groups began to resort to the federal courts more frequently than they had in the 1950s and 1960s.[9] This move was in part a reaction to the successes of liberal interest groups. Changes also resulted from the increasingly favorable forum that the federal courts provided for conservative viewpoints. The latter trend persisted throughout the 1980s because of President Ronald Reagan's success in placing judges on the federal bench who shared his conservative policy views.

In response, predominantly liberal interest groups began to seek forums other than the federal courts in which to pursue their policy goals. Some took their battles to the legislative branch, whereas others preferred to file suits in state courts.

Interest group involvement in the judicial process may take several different forms, depending on the goals of the particular group. Two principal tactics, however, stand out: involvement in test cases and presentation of information before the courts through amicus curiae briefs.

Test Cases

Because the judiciary engages in policymaking only by rendering decisions in specific cases, one favorite tactic of interest groups is to make sure that a case appropriate for obtaining its policy goals is brought before the court. In some instances the interest group initiates and sponsors the case by providing all the necessary resources. Undoubtedly the best-known example of this type of sponsorship may be found in *Brown v. Board of Education.*[10] Linda Brown, an African American, was denied admission to the public school nearest her home because that school was reserved for whites. Although the suit against the Board of Education of Topeka, Kansas, was filed by her parents, the NAACP supplied the legal help and money necessary to pursue the case all the way to the U.S. Supreme Court, where Thur-good Marshall (a future Supreme Court justice) argued the suit on behalf of the plaintiff and the NAACP. The NAACP gained a victory through the Supreme Court's decision that segregation in the public schools violates the equal protection clause of the Fourteenth Amendment.

Interest groups may also provide assistance in a case initiated by someone else but that raises issues of importance to the group. A good example is *Wisconsin v. Yoder,* which dealt with freedom of religion.[11] The state of Wisconsin filed criminal complaints charging Jonas Yoder and others with failure to send their children to school until the age of sixteen, as required by state law. Yoder and the others, members of the Amish sect, believed that education beyond the eighth grade led to the breakdown of values they cherished and to "worldly" influences on their children.

An organization known as the National Committee for Amish Religious Freedom (NCARF), which had been formed in 1965 by non-Amish ministers, bankers, lawyers, and professors to defend the right of the Amish to pursue their way of life, came to Yoder's defense. NCARF provided William R. Ball as defense attorney, as well as a number of expert witnesses who testified on behalf of the Amish.

Following a decision against the Amish in the trial court, NCARF appealed to a Wisconsin circuit court, which upheld the trial court's decision. An appeal was made to the Wisconsin Supreme Court, which ruled in favor of the Amish, saying that the compulsory school attendance law violated the First Amendment's free exercise clause. Wisconsin then appealed to the U.S. Supreme Court, which on May 15, 1972, sustained the religious objection that NCARF had raised to the compulsory school attendance laws.

Even though NCARF did not initiate the litigation, it found a test case and pursued it through four courts to obtain its objective. Without the actions of NCARF, the religious freedom interests of the Amish might not have been adequately presented, especially at the appellate level, because the Amish generally refused to defend themselves in litigation.

How extensive is interest-group sponsorship of cases? If one is referring to those cases that constitute ordinary litigation, the answer is that a very small proportion of them involve group sponsorship. Such sponsorship is, however, far more common in cases that have the potential to be heard by the Supreme Court and to produce a major legal ruling.[12]

The American Civil Liberties Union (ACLU), an organization dedicated to defending the Bill of Rights, is probably the interest group best known for sponsorship of cases in the nation's courts.[13] On the occasion of its seventieth anniversary in 1990, it was noted that "the ACLU had been involved in 80 percent of the post-1920 'landmark' cases regularly cited in constitutional law texts." [14]

The bulk of the literature on interest group involvement in litigation has focused on cases concerning major constitutional issues that have reached the Supreme Court. Because only a small percentage of cases ever reach the nation's highest court, however, much of the work of interest group lawyers deals with more routine work at the lower levels of the judiciary.

Instead of fashioning major test cases for the appellate courts, these attorneys may simply be required to deal with the legal problems of their groups' clientele.

A study of the routine activities of three litigation-oriented civil rights groups active in Mississippi in the mid-1960s provides some interesting insights.[15] For one thing, the authors of this study found that although the attorneys associated with the Lawyers Committee for Civil Rights under Law, the Lawyers Constitutional Defense Committee, and the NAACP Legal Defense Fund evidently preferred to litigate in the federal courts, most of their work was done in the state and local tribunals. The activities of these attorneys were wide-ranging. In addition to litigating major civil rights questions, they defended blacks and civil rights workers who encountered difficulties with the local authorities. These interest group attorneys, then, performed many of the functions of a specialized legal aid society.

Amicus Curiae Briefs

Submission of **amicus curiae** (friend of the court) briefs is the easiest method by which interest groups can become involved in cases. Consequently, it is also the most common form of group involvement. This method allows a group to get its message before the court even though it does not control the case. Provided it has the permission of the parties to the case or the permission of the court, an interest group may submit an amicus brief to supplement the arguments of the parties.

Sometimes these briefs are aimed at strengthening the position of one of the parties in the case. When *Wisconsin v. Yoder* was argued before the U.S. Supreme Court, the cause of the Amish was supported by amicus curiae briefs filed by the General Conference of Seventh Day Adventists, the National Council of Churches of Christ in the United States, the Synagogue Council of America, the American Jewish Congress, the National Jewish Commission on Law and Public Affairs, and the Mennonite Central Committee.[16] All supported exemption of the Amish from the compulsory school attendance laws.

Some cases attract amicus briefs supporting both parties in the case. Approximately 100 groups and individuals participated as amici curiae in *Lucas v. South Carolina Coastal Council.* A close examination reveals that "supporters of Lucas and the state matched constituency for constituency, at least in the areas of government, environment/public interest, and land use." [17]

Sometimes friend-of-the-court briefs are used not to strengthen the arguments of one of the parties but to suggest to the court the group's own view of how the case should be resolved. A classic example occurred in *Mapp v. Ohio.*[18] When that case was presented to the Supreme Court, the argument by the parties focused (1) on whether someone should be convicted for "mere possession" of obscene material, and (2) on the "shocking" nature of the search that led to the discovery of the material. Moreover, the defendant's lawyer did not urge a change in the ruling that improperly seized evidence could still be used in the trial. Instead, this issue was raised in the amicus curiae brief filed by the American Civil Liberties Union and the Ohio Civil Liberties Union.[19] The Supreme Court, without dealing with the obscenity issue, handed down a landmark constitutional decision excluding illegally seized evidence from trials in state courts (the exclusionary rule). It was the interest group's argument that provided the policy view adopted by the Supreme Court.

The filing of amicus curiae briefs is a tactic used in appellate rather than trial courts. Although the literature on friend-of-the-court participation deals most extensively with federal courts, amicus briefs may be filed in state appellate courts as well. Such filings have become especially more noticeable with the advent of "new judicial federalism." An examination of litigation activity in sixteen state supreme courts reveals not only a heightened presence of organized interests but also a wider range of groups participating as amici curiae.[20] Furthermore, findings indicate that "business groups, other organizational players, and even individual amici appear to be quite successful." [21] One specific way that amici curiae can be helpful in state supreme court cases is to intervene in support of a position advocated by an individual with a relatively low level of resources.[22]

SUMMARY

Our focus in this chapter was on three important actors in the judicial process: lawyers, litigants, and interest groups. Singled out for special emphasis were the government lawyers and the private attorneys who are primarily involved in handling cases in the state trial and appellate courts.

We next turned our attention to those who become litigants in state courts. The adversaries may be ordinary litigants who are primarily concerned with being compensated for their losses. Or the combatants are involved in political litigation and have as their major goal influencing public policy. Still other cases feature litigants who are interested in both personal compensation and exerting some influence over public policy.

We concluded with an examination of the role of interest groups in the judicial process. Following a brief look at the reasons groups become involved in litigation, we discussed the major strategies and tactics used by interest groups in the judicial arena: involvement in test cases and the use of amicus curiae briefs.

FURTHER THOUGHT AND DISCUSSION QUESTIONS

1. Given their importance in American society and government, why are lawyers so unpopular?

2. How can a system that claims to be unbiased and impartial allow interest-group participation in the judicial process?

Notes

1. See James Eisenstein and Herbert Jacob, *Felony Justice* (Boston: Little, Brown, 1977).
2. Howard Abadinsky, *Law and Justice*, 2nd ed. (Chicago: Nelson-Hall, 1991), 201.
3. Our brief account is drawn from Rorie J. Spill, Michael J. Licari, and Leonard Ray, "Taking on Tobacco: Policy Entrepreneurship and the Tobacco Litigation," *Political Research Quarterly* 54 (September 2001): 605–622.
4. Paul Wice, *Criminal Lawyers: An Endangered Species* (Beverly Hills, Calif.: Sage, 1978).
5. Our discussion of legal clinics and prepaid legal plans is drawn from Steven Vago, *Law and Society*, 8th ed. (Upper Saddle River, N.J.: Pearson Prentice Hall, 2006), 391–392.
6. Phillip J. Cooper, *Hard Judicial Choices* (New York: Oxford University Press, 1988), 13.
7. See Bob Van Voris, "The Torts of Summer," www.law.com.
8. *Lucas v. South Carolina Coastal Council*, 505 U.S. 1003 (1992).
9. See Karen O'Connor and Lee Epstein, "The Rise of Conservative Interest Group Litigation," *Journal of Politics* 45 (May 1983): 479–489; and Lee Epstein, *Conservatives in Court* (Knoxville: University of Tennessee Press, 1985).
10. *Brown v. Board of Education*, 347 U.S. 483 (1954).
11. *Wisconsin v. Yoder*, 406 U.S. 205 (1972). See also the excellent discussion of this case in Richard C. Cortner, *The Supreme Court and Civil Liberties Policy* (Palo Alto, Calif.: Mayfield, 1975), 153–182. Our discussion is based on this study.
12. See Lawrence Baum, *The Supreme Court*, 9th ed. (Washington, D.C.: CQ Press, 2007), 78.
13. For a complete history of the American Civil Liberties Union, see Samuel Walker, *In Defense of American Liberties: A History of the ACLU* (New York: Oxford University Press, 1990).
14. Ibid., 371.
15. See Joseph Stewart Jr. and Edward V. Heck, "The Day-to-Day Activities of Interest Group Lawyers," *Social Science Quarterly* 64 (March 1983): 173–182.
16. See Cortner, *The Supreme Court and Civil Liberties Policy*, 169–170.
17. Lee Epstein and Thomas G. Walker, *Constitutional Law for a Changing America: Institutional Powers and Constraints*, 4th ed. (Washington, D.C.: CQ Press, 2001), 45.
18. *Mapp v. Ohio*, 367 U.S. 643 (1961).
19. See Stephen L. Wasby, *The Supreme Court in the Federal Judicial System*, 3rd ed. (Chicago: Nelson Hall, 1988), 151–152.
20. Lee Epstein, "Exploring the Participation of Organized Interests in State Court Litigation," *Political Research Quarterly* 47 (June 1994): 335–351.
21. Donald R. Songer and Ashlyn Kuersten, "The Success of Amici in State Supreme Courts," *Political Research Quarterly* 48 (March 1995): 40.
22. See Donald R. Songer, Ashlyn Kuersten, and Erin Kaheny, "Why the Haves Don't Always Come Out Ahead: Repeat Players Meet Amici Curiae for the Disadvantaged," *Political Research Quarterly* 53 (September 2000): 552.

SUGGESTED RESOURCES

American Bar Association. Available online at www.abanet.org. Useful information for lawyers, students, and the general public.

American Bar Association Law Information. Available online at www.abalawinfo.org. An excellent source of information on varied aspects of law. Designed with consumers in mind.

Cortner, Richard C. *The Supreme Court and Civil Liberties Policy*. Palo Alto, Calif.: Mayfield, 1975. Case studies of several major Supreme Court decisions and how they evolved through the judicial system.

Eisenstein, James, and Herbert Jacob. *Felony Justice*. Boston: Little, Brown, 1977. The authors describe the courtroom work group and its role in the processing of felony criminal cases.

Walker, Samuel E. *In Defense of American Liberties: A History of the ACLU*. New York: Oxford University Press, 1991. A detailed historical analysis of one of the interest groups most frequently involved in the American judicial system.

Robert A. Carp, Ronald Stidham, and Kenneth L. Manning, *The State Courts,* (Washington, DC: CQ Press, 2010).

6. DECISION MAKING BY STATE COURT JUDGES

On what basis and for what reasons do judges in the United States rule the way they do on the motions, petitions, and judicial policy questions that require their attention? In this chapter we respond to this question by summarizing the theories and research findings of a large number of judicial scholars who have tried to find out what makes judges tick. We examine state jurists as a group because, to a large extent, the variables that influence judicial decision making are the same for judges at both trial and appellate levels. Both types of judges tend to be governed strongly by court precedents, and virtually all judges reflect to some degree their political party affiliation.

It is useful to begin with a brief discussion of the decision-making environment in which trial judges and their appellate colleagues operate. Because of the differing purposes and organizational frameworks of trial and appellate courts, judges of each type face particular kinds of pressure and expectations. As described by Richard J. Richardson and Kenneth N. Vines, all jurists are, however, subject to two major kinds of influence: the legal subculture and the democratic subculture.[1] In any given case, it is often difficult to determine the relative impact of a specific influence on a judge. Studies have suggested that when judges, especially trial judges, find no significant precedent to guide them—that is, when the legal subculture cupboard is bare—they tend to turn to the democratic subculture, an amalgam of determinants that includes their own political inclinations.

At the base of the state judicial hierarchies are the trial court judges, who preside over the judicial process and corporately make hundreds of millions of decisions each year. Some decisions pertain to legal points and procedures raised by litigants even before a trial begins, such as a motion by a criminal defendant's lawyer to exclude from trial a piece of illegally obtained evidence. During the trial a judge must rule on scores of motions made by the attorneys in the case, such as an objection to a particular question asked of a witness or a request to strike contested testimony from the record. Even after a verdict has been rendered, a trial judge may be confronted with demands for decisions; a litigant's request to reduce a monetary award made by a civil jury is an example.

Trial judges can and occasionally do take ample time to reflect on the more important decisions and may consult with their staff or other judges about how to handle a particular legal problem. Nevertheless, a significant portion of their decision making must be done on the spur of the moment, without the luxury of lengthy reflection or discussion with staff or colleagues. As one trial judge told us, "We're where the action is. We often have to 'shoot from the hip' and hope you're doing the right thing. You can't ruminate forever every time you have to make a ruling. We'd be spending months on each case if we ever did that." (Virtually all of the judges interviewed for this study were promised anonymity.)

Decision making by the appeals courts and the supreme courts is different in several important respects. By the time a case reaches the appellate level, the record and facts have already been established. The jurists' job is to review dispassionately the transcript of a trial that has already occurred, to search for legal errors that may have been committed by others. Few snap judgments are required. And although the appeals courts and a supreme court may occasionally hear oral arguments by attorneys, they do not examine witnesses and they are removed from the drama and confrontations of the trial courtroom. Another difference in the decision-making process is that the trial level is largely individualistic, whereas the appellate level is to some degree the product of group deliberation.

Despite the acknowledged differences between trial and appellate judge decision making, all American jurists have many values in common. We examine several studies that have sought to explain why judges think and act as they do, using Richardson and Vines's basic analytic framework. The thrust of these scholarly efforts has differed. Some view judges as judicial computers who take in a volume of facts, law, and legal doctrines and spew out "correct" rulings—determinations that are virtually independent of the judges' values and characteristics as human beings. Other researchers tend to explain judicial decision making in terms of the personal orientations of the judges. A decision is seen not so much as the product of an unbiased, exacting thought process that judges learn in law school; rather, it is seen as having been affected by the judge's life experiences, prejudices, and overall social values. As with most theories of human behavior, each of these approaches has its fair share of the truth, but none provides the whole story.

THE LEGAL SUBCULTURE

It is useful in examining the legal subculture as a source of trial judge decision making to focus on a number of specific questions. What are the basic rules, practices, and norms of this subculture? Where do judges learn these principles, and what groups or institutions keep judges from departing from them? How often and under what circumstances do judges respond to stimuli other than those from the traditional legal realm?

The Nature of Legal Reasoning

In a popular television series of the 1970s, *The Paper Chase,* the formidable Professor Kingsfield promises his budding law students that if they work hard and entrust their mush-filled brains to him, he will instill in them the ability "to think like a lawyer." How do lawyers and judges think when they deliberate in their professional capacities? One classic answer to this question is that "the basic pattern of legal reasoning is reasoning by example. It is a three-step process described by the doctrine of precedent as follows: (1) similarity is seen between cases; (2) the rule of law inherent in the first case is announced; and (3) the rule of law is made applicable to the second case." [2]

Two cases, *Lane v. Wilson* and *Gomillion v. Lightfoot,* had similar arguments and factual situations.[3] In *Lane,* a black citizen of Oklahoma brought suit in federal court, alleging that he had been deprived of the right to vote. In 1916 the legislature of that state had passed a law, ostensibly designed to give formerly disenfranchised black citizens the right to vote, that required them to register—but the registration period lasted only twelve days. (White voters were for all practical purposes exempted from this scheme through the use of a "grandfather clause.") If blacks did not sign up within that short interval, never again would they have the right to vote. The Oklahoma legislature clearly realized that a twelve-day period was wholly inadequate for blacks to mount a voter registration drive and that the vast majority would not acquire the franchise. The plaintiff in this case did not get on the registration rolls in 1916. When he was thereafter forbidden to vote, he brought suit, claiming that the Oklahoma registration scheme was unconstitutional. The Supreme Court agreed with the plaintiff. In striking down the statute, it set forth this principle, or rule of law: "The Fifteenth Amendment nullifies sophisticated as well as simple-minded modes of discrimination." [4]

Two decades later another black citizen, Charles Gomillion, brought suit in the federal courts, alleging a denial of his right to vote as secured by the Fifteenth Amendment. Here an Alabama statute altered the Tuskegee city boundaries from a square to a twenty-eight-sided figure, allegedly removing "all save only four or five of its 400 Negro voters while not removing a single white voter or resident." Although not denying a legislature's right to alter city boundaries "under normal circumstances," the Court saw through the Alabama legislature's thinly disguised attempt to deny suffrage to the black citizens of Tuskegee. Reasoning that the situation in *Gomillion* was analogous to that in the Oklahoma case, the Court used the precedent of *Lane v. Wilson* to strike down the Alabama law: "It is difficult to appreciate what stands in the way of adjudging a statute having this inevitable effect invalid in light of the principles of which this Court must judge, and uniformly has judged, statutes that, howsoever speciously defined, obviously discriminate against colored citizens. 'The Fifteenth Amendment nullifies sophisticated as well as simple-minded modes of discrimination.' *Lane v. Wilson.*" [5] This opinion is one example of the judicial reasoning process—of thinking like Professor Kingsfield's lawyer. Two cases are compared because the facts or principles are similar; a rule of law gleaned from the first case is applied to the second. This step-by-step process is the essence of proper and traditional legal reasoning.

Adherence to Precedent

A related value held by trial and appellate judges is a commitment to follow precedents—decisions rendered on similar subjects by judges in the past. The sacred doctrine of ***stare decisis*** ("stand by what has been decided") is a cardinal principle of the common law tradition. In a recent national survey of more than 1,000 trial court judges in the United States, the jurists were asked about how important precedent was in their decision making—especially when the precedent was "clear and directly relevant." Ninety-one percent replied that it was "very important." By contrast, when these same jurists were asked to rate the importance of their own personal "view of justice in the case," only 28 percent said that was "very important."[6]

Constraints on Trial Judge Decision Making

Another significant element of the legal subculture is found under the heading of what one prominent scholar has called the "great maxims of judicial self-restraint."[1] These maxims derive from a variety of sources—the common law, statutory law, legal tradition—but each serves to limit and channel the decision making of state judges. We now look at a few of the major themes of judicial self-restraint.

Before a judge will agree to consider a lawsuit, a definite case or controversy at law or in equity must exist between bona fide adversaries under the Constitution. The case must concern the protection or enforcement of valuable legal rights or the punishment, prevention, or redress of wrongs directly related to the litigants. Allied with this maxim is the principle that U.S. judges may not render advisory opinions, that is, rulings on abstract, hypothetical questions. (This rule is not followed as strictly in many state systems.) Also, all parties to a lawsuit must have standing, or a substantial personal interest infringed on by the statute or action in question.

The rules of the game forbid jurists to hear a case unless all other legal remedies have been exhausted. In addition, the legal culture discourages the judiciary from deciding political questions or matters that ought to be resolved by one of the other branches of government, by another level of government, or by the voters. Judges are obliged to give the benefit of the doubt to statutes and official actions when their constitutionality is being questioned. A law or an executive action is presumed to be constitutional until proven otherwise. (Some judges adhere to this principle on economic issues but not on matters of civil rights and civil liberties, believing that in these matters the burden of proof is on the government.) In this same realm, judges feel bound by the norm that if a law must be invalidated, they will do so on as narrow a ground as possible or will void only that portion of the statute that is unconstitutional.

Finally, American jurists may not throw out a law or an official action simply because they personally believe it is unfair, stupid, or undemocratic. For a statute or an official deed to be invalidated, it must clearly be unconstitutional. Judges do not always agree about what is a clearly unconstitutional act, but most acknowledge that broad matters of public policy should be determined by the people through their elected representatives—not by the judiciary.

The Impact of the Legal Subculture: An Example

Because the principles that make up the legal subculture—reasoning, precedent, and restraint—tend to be abstract, it is useful to illustrate them with a real-life example. *Evers v. Jackson Municipal Separate School District* was an uncomplicated 1964 school integration case in which a group of black children and their parents sought to enjoin the "district and its officials from operating a compulsory biracial school system."[2] The facts and controlling precedents were clear: (1) Jackson, Mississippi, was overtly maintaining a segregated public school system; (2) the U.S. Supreme Court had ruled a decade earlier, in *Brown v. Board of Education,* that such segregation was unconstitutional; and (3) the U.S. Court of Appeals for the Fifth Circuit, which has jurisdiction over Mississippi, had handed down a string of rulings ordering the integration process to go forward.

Sidney Mize, the federal trial judge in *Evers,* did not like the commands he heard from the legal subculture. Appointed to the federal bench in 1937, Mize was an unabashed segregationist, as his written opinion in this case clearly shows. After discussing a score of alleged physical and mental differences between blacks and whites, Mize argued further that

> in the case of Caucasians and Negroes, such differences may be directly confirmed by comparative anatomical and encephalographic measurements of the correlative physical structure of the brain and of the neural and endocrine systems of the body. The evidence was conclusive to the effect that the cranial capacity and brain size of the average Negro is approximately ten per cent less than that of the average

> white person of similar age and size, and that brain size is correlated with intelligence.[3]

Judge Mize also argued, "From the evidence I find that separate classes allow greater adaptation to the differing educational traits of Negro and white pupils, and actually result in greater scholastic accomplishments for both."[4]

It seems clear where this decision was headed. Enter the legal subculture. After fourteen single-spaced printed pages of argument against the integration of the Jackson schools, Mize yielded to the requirements of legal reasoning, respect for precedent, and judicial self-restraint. Almost sheepishly he concluded his decision with these unexpected words:

> Nevertheless, this Court feels that it is bound by what appears to be the obvious holding of the United States Court of Appeals for the Fifth Circuit that if disparities and differences such as that reflected in this record are to constitute a proper basis for the maintenance of separate schools for the white and Negro races it is the function of the United States Supreme Court to make such a decision and no inferior federal court can do so.[5]

Mize then quietly enjoined the school district and its officials from operating a compulsory biracial school system. The legal subculture tiptoed to victory.

Wellsprings of the Legal Subculture

The institutions that instill and maintain the legal values in the United States are "the law schools, the bar associations, the judicial councils, and other groups that spring from the institutionalization of the 'bench and the bar.' "[6]

"The purpose of law school," a scholar wrote, "is to change people; to turn them into novice lawyers; and to instill in them a nascent self-concept as a professional, a commitment to the value of the calling, and a claim to that elusive and esoteric style of reasoning called 'thinking like a lawyer.' "[7] The world just does not look the same to someone on whom law school has worked its indoctrinating magic. Facts and relationships in the human arena that formerly went unnoticed suddenly become "compelling" and "controlling" to the fledgling advocate. Likewise, other facets of reality that previously had been important in one's worldview are now dismissed as "irrelevant and immaterial."

Besides the indoctrination that occurs in law school, the values of the legal subculture are maintained by the state and national bar associations and by a variety of professional-social groups whose members are from both bench and bar, such as the honorary Order of the Coif.[8] The values and practices of jurists are handed down from one generation to another. In this way, the traditions and tenets of the American legal subculture are well tended by powerful support groups. They are rightly accorded ample deference if one is to understand judicial decision making in America.

The Limits of the Legal Subculture

Despite the taut nature of judicial reasoning and the importance of *stare decisis* and judicial self-restraint, the legal subculture does not totally explain the behavior of American jurists. If objective facts and obvious controlling precedents were the only stimuli to which jurists responded, the judicial decision-making process would be largely mechanical, and all judicial outcomes would be predictable. Yet even the legal subculture's most loyal apologists would concede that judges often distinguish between precedents and that some judges are more inclined than others toward self-restraint.

To understand the thinking of judicial decision makers and the evolution of the law, it is necessary to consider more than law school curricula and the canons of the bar associations. One of the first great minds to realize this was Justice Oliver Wendell Holmes Jr., who more than a century ago wrote:

> [T]he life of the law has not been logic; it has been experience. The felt necessities of the time, the prevalent moral and political theories, intuitions of public policy, avowed or unconscious, even the prejudices which judges share with their fellow-men have had a good deal more to do than syllogism in determining the rules by which men should be governed. The law embodies the story of a nation's development through many centuries, and it cannot be dealt with as if it contained only the axioms and corollaries of a book of mathematics. In order to know what it is, we must know what it has been, and what it tends to become.... The very considerations which judges most rarely mention, and always with an apology, are the secret root from which the law draws all the juices of life. I mean, of course, considerations of what is expedient for the community concerned.[9]

By about the 1920s an entire school of thought had developed that argued that judicial decision making is as much the product of human, extralegal stimuli as it is of some sort of mechanical legal thought process. Adherents of this view, who were known as **judicial realists,** insisted that judges, like other human beings, are influenced by the values and attitudes learned in childhood. As one of these realists put it, a judge's background "may have created plus or minus reactions to women, or blonde women, or men with beards, or Southerners, or Italians, or Englishmen, or plumbers, or ministers, or college graduates, or Democrats. A certain facial twitch or cough or gesture may start up memories, painful or pleasant."[10]

Since the late 1940s, the study of the personal, extralegal influences on decision making has become more rigorous. Often calling themselves judicial behavioralists, modern-day advocates of the realist approach have improved on it in two ways. First, they have tried to test empirically many of the theories and propositions advanced by the realist school. Second, they have attempted to relate their findings to more scientifically grounded theories of human behavior. A realist might have asserted that a Democratic judge would probably be more supportive of labor unions than a Republican jurist would be, but a judicial behavioralist might go a step further by taking a generous random sample of labor-union-versus-management decisions and statistically determining whether Democratic judges are significantly more likely than their GOP counterparts to back the union. It is one thing to intuitively ascribe a cause for human behavior; it is another to subject an assertion to careful empirical analysis.

THE DEMOCRATIC SUBCULTURE

Evidence shows that popular democratic values—manifested in a variety of ways through many different mediums—have an influence as well, just as the legal subculture does. Some scholars have argued that the only reason courts have maintained their significance in the American political system is that they learned to bend when the democratic winds blow. In other words, judges have tempered rigid legalisms with commonsense popular values and have maintained "extensive linkages with the democratic subculture."

In discussing the democratic subculture, we focus on the influences most often observed by students of the American court system—political party identification, localism, public opinion, and the legislative and executive branches of government.

The Influence of Political Party Affiliation

Do the political party affiliations of judges affect the way they decide certain cases? The question is straightforward enough, but the responses are by no means in unanimous agreement. To most attorneys, judges, and court watchers among the general public, the question sounds impertinent, and their answer is usually something like this: After taking the judicial oath and donning the black robe, a judge is no longer a Republican or a Democrat. Former affiliations are (or at least certainly should be) put aside as the judge enters a realm in which decisions are the product of evidence, sound judicial reasoning, and precedent, as opposed to such a base factor as political identification. Or, as Donald Dale Jackson quipped in his perceptive book *Judges*, "Most judges would sooner admit to grand larceny than confess a political interest or motivation." [11]

Despite the cries of indignation from those who contend that the legal subculture explains virtually all judicial decision making, a mounting body of evidence strongly suggests that judges' political identification does affect their behavior on the bench.[12] One prominent student of American politics explains why there may be a cause-and-effect relationship between judges' party allegiance and their decisional patterns:

> If judges are party identifiers before reaching the bench, there would be a basis for believing that they—like legislators—are affected in their issue orientations by party.... Furthermore, judges are generally well educated and the vote studies show that the more educated tend to be stronger party identifiers, to cast policy preferences in ideological terms, to have clearer perceptions of issues and of party positions on those issues, to have issue attitudes consistent with the positions of the party with which they identify, and to be more interested and involved in politics. For judges, even more than for the general population, party may therefore be a significant reference group on issues.[13]

Partisanship in State Courts.

Partisan voting patterns often occur among the men and women who sit on the trial and appellate court benches. The evidence at the state level is, however, weaker than at the federal level, for three general reasons. First, the state courts have not been studied as extensively and systematically as the federal courts. The reason may be that some political scientists have held the (mistaken) view that state judiciaries are less important than their federal counterparts or that many state court decisions are unpublished and therefore more difficult to obtain and study. Second, partisanship among state jurists is not strongly uniform across the country. In some states, judicial selection is truly bipartisan (or nonpartisan), and both political parties may support the same candidates. Also, many state judges do not have extensive relationships with a political party. Although they may have partisan identifications, they may not view judicial questions as being reflective of their party's ideology. Finally, because America still has a number of one-party states in which virtually all judges bear the same party label, it would make little sense to study partisan differences among judges in these states. Nevertheless, keen levels of partisanship have been documented in some jurisdictions—particularly in the states with big cities.

Partisan voting patterns among judges in Michigan have been noteworthy, especially on the state supreme court. Studies have shown that on labor-management issues, Democrats on the bench were significantly more likely to support the side of the worker in unemployment compensation cases and in issues dealing with workers' compensation (on-the-job injuries). Democratic judges are also more likely to support criminal defendants seeking a new trial, to favor government efforts to regulate business, and to side with persons who sue business enterprises—all consistent with the voting behavior of Democrats on the federal bench.[14]

In a study of partisan conflict on a California intermediate court of appeals, significant differences were found between Democrats and Republicans in criminal and civil cases.[15] Studying the votes in criminal justice cases, labor-management disputes, debtor-creditor disagreements, and consumerism, the author concluded that "as previous research … would have predicted, the results are in the expected direction, with Republican panels significantly more likely to reach conservative outcomes than Democratic panels." [16] Illinois, Iowa, Maryland, New York, and Pennsylvania are examples of other states where researchers have found meaningful partisan differences between Republican and Democratic judges.[17]

Finally, a recent comprehensive study of state supreme court chief justices found "a significant relationship between citizen ideology and the ideology of the chief justice." [18] That is, the partisan values of a majority of a state's voters is often reflected in corresponding partisan behavior by the state's supreme court chief justice.

An Appraisal.

The political party affiliation of the judges and justices can make a difference in the way they decide cases. Of all the background variables studied, party affiliation seems to be the most compelling and consistent. But a word of caution is in order. Although evidence of partisan influence on judicial behavior is convincing, it by no means suggests that Democrats always take the liberal position on all issues and Republicans always opt for the conservative side. Rather, it is a matter of tendencies. When the decision is a close call, a Democrat on the bench tends to be more **liberal** than a Republican judge. When controlling precedents are absent or ambiguous or when the evidence in the case is about evenly divided, Democrats are more inclined than Republicans to support civil rights and liberties, to support government regulation that favors the worker or the economic underdog, and to turn a sympathetic ear toward the pleas of criminal defendants.

The Impact of Localism

A wide range of influences are included in the term *localism*, and we regard it as a broad second category of factors that affect state judicial decision making. For trial and appeals court judges, geographic differences define both the legal and the democratic subcultures as well as the nature of the questions they must decide. Historically, such judges have had strong ties to the state and the region in which their courts are situated, and on many issues judicial decision making reflects the parochial values and attitudes of the region.

Localism and the Behavior of State Judges.

State judges tend to be local folks—born, bred, educated, and socialized in the locale in which they preside. Whether they have been elected directly by the people or appointed as a result of their political connections with the governor or the local political machine, state judges are likely to mirror the values and attitudes of their environment. A study by Martin A. Levin, who compared and contrasted judges and justices in Minneapolis and Pittsburgh, provides a fitting example.[19]

In Minneapolis the state trial judges are elected on a nonpartisan ballot, and in practice the political parties have almost no role in the selection of judges. "The socialization and recruitment of [the] … judges reflect this pattern of selection. Most of these judges [like the majority of the local population] have Northern European-Protestant and middle-class backgrounds, and their pre-judicial careers have been predominantly in private legal practice …. Such career experiences seem to have stimulated these judges to be interested more in 'society' than in the defendant." [20] Minneapolis's conservative, middle-class environment, from which its judges come, is reflected in the law-and-order, no-nonsense grist of the judicial mill:

> This pre-judicial experience, reinforced by their lack of party or policy-oriented experiences and their middle-class backgrounds, seems to have contributed to the legalistic and universalistic character of their decision-making and their eschewal of policy and personal considerations. In their milieu, rules were generally emphasized, especially legal ones, and these rules had been used to maintain and protect societal institutions. Learning to "get around" involved skill in operating in a context of rules. The judges' success seems to have depended more on their objective achievements and skills than on personal relationships.[21]

The environment of the Pittsburgh jurists is in stark contrast. The highly partisan (Democratic) judges reflect the working-class, ethnic group-based values of the political machine that put them on the bench. They were likely to have held public office before becoming judges and, as a result, were much more people-oriented than their counterparts in Minneapolis. They often felt that their own "minority ethnic and lower-income backgrounds and these government and party experiences had developed their general attachment to the problems of the 'underdog' and the 'oppressed.' " Levin makes the following conclusion about the impact of the local environment and recruitment process on judicial behavior:

> Their political experiences and lack of much legalistic experience apparently contributed to the highly particularistic and nonlegalistic character of their decision-making, their emphasis on policy considerations, and their use of pragmatic criteria.... Personal relationships, especially with constituents, were emphasized, and focused on particular and tangible entities. Success depended largely on the ability to operate within personal relationships. It depended on whom one knew, rather than on what one knew. Abstractions such as "the good of society as a whole" seem to have been of little concern.[22]

Although social science still needs to develop more systematic empirical evidence for the relationship between the local environment and the output of state courts, these two brief case studies are indicative of the kind of phenomena we are describing.

The Impact of Public Opinion

If one were to approach a typical judge or justice and ask whether public opinion affected the decisions made from the bench, the jurist might respond with a fair measure of indignation. The answer might be something like this: "Look, as a judge with a lifetime appointment, I'm expected to be free from the pressures of public opinion. That's part of what we mean when we say that we're a 'government of laws—not of men.' When I decide a case, I look at the law and the facts. I don't go out into the streets and take some sort of public opinion poll to tell me what to do."

Yet to some degree and on certain issues, American judges do seem to temper their decision making with public opinion. There are several intuitive reasons for this. First, judges, as human beings, as parents, as consumers, and as residents of the community, are themselves part of public opinion. Putting on a black robe may stimulate a greater concern for responsible, objective decision making, but it does not void a judge's membership in the human race. As one judicial scholar has noted, "Since judges, both appointed and elected, usually have been born and reared locally and recruited from a local political system, it seems likely that public opinion would have an effect, especially in issues that are locally visible and controversial. In addition … many judges seem to consider themselves independent judicial officials who represent local populations in the courts. Consequently, judges may feel that they ought to take local values into account." 23

The empirical evidence for the impact of public opinion is suggestive but hardly conclusive, in part because relatively few comprehensive studies of the phenomenon have been conducted and the proposition is difficult to prove. Many of the earliest studies of this subject produced conflicting conclusions, but more recent and exhaustive investigations have begun to map a real, albeit imperfect, relationship between public opinion and jurists' decisional patterns.[24]

Some researchers have explored this phenomenon at the state level. A study of California state courts found that the severity of sentencing in marijuana cases began to change soon after a popular referendum was held on reducing criminal penalties for personal use of the drug. Judges who had given light sentences before the referendum sometimes gave harsher sentences if the local vote was in favor of maintaining criminal penalties. Conversely, harsh-sentencing jurists sometimes became more lenient when the vote indicated that the public favored reducing the penalties.[25]

Given that in a majority of states judges must periodically run for election, they probably are more attuned to public opinion than are federal judges, who have lifetime tenure. One study of elected state supreme court justices found that "to appease their constituencies, justices who have views contrary to those of the voters and the court majority, and who face competitive electoral conditions will vote with the court majority instead of casting unpopular dissents on politically volatile issues."[26] Likewise, a more recent study involving state supreme court justices' voting behavior in death penalty cases found a clear link between their voting patterns and voter sentiment about capital punishment. The authors noted that "on the highly salient issue of the death penalty, mass opinion and the institution of electing judges systematically influence composition and judge behavior." [27]

The following more down-to-earth example illustrates a state judge's stronger grassroots political awareness and the greater degree to which elected jurists interact with the local environment. On November 28, 1988, Jack Hampton, a state district court judge in Dallas, gave a thirty-year prison sentence to a defendant who had been convicted of murdering two gay men. The killer, Richard Bednarski, had testified in court that he and some friends went to a central Dallas park to "pester homosexuals" and ended up killing two of them in what authorities called an execution-style slaying. (Bednarski placed a gun in one victim's mouth and pulled the trigger; he then shot the other man several times.) Because of the heinous and unprovoked nature of the crime and because Hampton is known as a "hanging judge" who usually gives life sentences for murder, the *Dallas Times Herald* decided to interview the judge about his lighter than usual sentence. During the interview Judge Hampton said that the murder victims more or less got what they asked for, because they were "queers" who "wouldn't have been killed if they hadn't been cruising the streets picking up teenage boys." [28]

Immediately after the interview was published, public protests were staged by human rights groups, local church leaders, and various gay rights organizations. Protest rallies were held, including one attended by 500 people at the City Hall Plaza, where letters of support were read from Sen. Edward M. Kennedy of Massachusetts and Texas state treasurer Ann Richards. Also, formal complaints were filed with the Texas Commission on Judicial Conduct, calling for Hampton to be disciplined. In reply, this elected judicial official issued a four-paragraph letter to a group of eight Methodist ministers. Judge Hampton said he wished "to apologize" for his "poor choice of words that appeared in a recent newspaper story." He promised that in his court "everyone is entitled to and will receive equal protection."

Was the judge's public apology a response to his perception of public opinion and its possible effect on his bid for reelection? This conclusion might be surmised from the judge's later statement, responding to a question about the possible political fallout from the incident: "If it makes anybody mad, they'll forget it by 1990" (when Judge Hampton was up for reelection).[29] He was reelected.

This particular incident is not typical of the behavior of state judges, but it demonstrates the degree to which locally elected judicial officials respond to the tides of public opinion. Very rarely do lifetime judicial appointees, such as federal judges, feel the need to justify their sentencing behavior in interviews with the local press or to issue public apologies when public opinion turns critical of their behavior. For better or worse, public opinion does affect judicial behavior, and particularly when judges must be accountable directly to the electorate.

Despite the traditional notion of the blindfolded justice weighing only the facts in a case and the relevant law, common sense and statistical evidence support the assertion that jurists do keep their eyes (and ears) open to public opinion.

The Influence of the State Legislature and the Governor

In almost half of the jurisdictions the popularly elected governor (or the state legislature) selects the state judges, and a policy link is likely to exist among the value sets of the voters, the appointing officials, and the judges who render subsequent decisions. When Texas governor Rick Perry met privately with a group of Dallas school officials in 2004, he candidly "predicted … that a lawsuit challenging the state school finance law [would] fail because his appointees to the Texas Supreme Court [would not] force changes on the Legislature." As the former president of the Highland Park (Dallas) school board said in response to the governor's comments, "He didn't say he had spoken to them [the justices], but I just couldn't believe it, and a lot of other people couldn't believe it either. They were stunned that a governor would say something like that." [30] (As it happened, the governor's prediction was accurate, because the state supreme court did not overturn the law in question.)

More specifically, the authors of one study found three major ways in which the political branches affect the role of the state courts.[31] First, legislation sponsored by the governor or passed by the legislature regulates the types of claims that can be adjudicated in state courts and also brought to the state appellate courts. For example, class action suits may be easily brought in state judicial tribunals. Actions by the legislature determine who may bring such suits and under what circumstances. The evidence suggests that the states vary greatly in this area. Some states make it easy to initiate such suits, whereas in others access to the courts is difficult.[32]

Second, actions by the legislature (which may or may not be part of the governor's political agenda) determine the authority of the state supreme court to regulate its workload and focus on important cases. It is generally accepted that for most cases litigants should have the right to appeal trial court decisions. In states that have an ample number of intermediate appellate courts this right to appeal is readily available, but in states without a sufficient number of intermediate appeals courts or in states where the supreme court is forced by law to deal with a succession of relatively minor disputes, the chances are slim that litigants will have their cases heard by the supreme court. This fact is significant in terms of the distribution of justice, and it is also important for another reason. In states where the legislature forces the supreme court to overwork on judicial trivia, the court does not have time to devote much attention to cases that raise important policy questions. A study concluded that after the North Carolina legislature created intermediate courts of appeals, the state supreme court was able to assume "a position of true leadership in the legal development of the state." [33] Therefore, actions by the legislature (supported or opposed by the governor) may determine whether the supreme court plays a major or a minor role in policy questions important to the state.

Finally, because a prime function of courts is to enforce existing legal norms, the sorts of issues that state courts address depend to a large degree on the substantive law of the state. Seventeen state constitutions contain "little ERAs" (equal rights amendments); ten states specifically protect the right to privacy; and some states guarantee a right to quality of the environment.[34] A judge in a state where good air quality is guaranteed will have a much greater opportunity and right to issue an injunction against a polluter than will the judge in a state where such a right is not legally provided. One area in which legislatures have taken an issue out of the hands of state judges is gay and lesbian rights. After the courts began to hand down decisions favoring such rights, including *Lawrence v. Texas*[35], some thirty state legislatures adopted state constitutional amendments that defined marriage as between a man and a woman.[36] These amendments in effect preclude judges in these thirty states from handing down a ruling in favor of same-sex marriage that is based on these states' laws or constitutions. The point is that judges render decisions within the existing constitutional and legal environment of their respective states. Such an environment is largely the product of political decisions made by the governor and the legislature as representatives of the electorate.

In sum, the output of the state courts is to a significant degree the result of the political values and policy goals of the chief executive and the legislative branch of government.

THE SUBCULTURES AS PREDICTORS

Scholarly opinion differs on whether judicial decision making is essentially the product of facts, laws, and precedent (the legal subculture model) or whether the various extralegal factors carry more weight (the realist-behavioralist view). In other words, are court decisions better explained by understanding the facts and law that impinge on a given case or by knowing which newspaper the judge reads in the morning or how the judge voted in the last election?

The clue to answering the question lies in knowing what kind of case the judge is being asked to decide. The vast majority of state trial judges' cases and much appellate judicial business involve routine norm enforcement decisions. In cases in which the law and the controlling precedents are clear, the victor will be the side that is able to marshal better evidence to show that its factual case is stronger. In other words, in the lion's share of cases, the legal subculture model best explains and predicts judicial decision making. When traditional legal cues are ambiguous or absent, however, judges are obliged to look to the democratic subculture for guidance in their decision making. We think that Illinois senator (now president) Barack Obama got pretty close to the truth in a 2005 speech dealing with judicial appointments. Obama argued that 95 percent of court cases are easily settled on the basis of the law and precedent. But in "those 5 percent of hard cases the legal process alone will not lead you to a rule of decision and the critical ingredient is supplied by what is in the judge's heart." [37]

When the Legal Evidence Is Contradictory

It is probably fair to say that in a majority of cases the facts, evidence, and controlling precedents distinctly favor one side. In such instances the judge is clearly obliged to decide for the party with the stronger case. Not to do so would violate the judge's legal training and mores; subject a trial or appeals court judge to reversal by a higher court, an event most jurists find embarrassing; and render the supreme court vulnerable to the charge that it was making up the law as it went along—an impression not flattering to the high court justices. But judges often find themselves in situations in which the facts and evidence are about equally compelling on both sides, or in which a roughly equal number of precedents sustain a finding for either party. As one U.S. trial judge in Houston told us,

> There are days when you want to say to the litigants, "I wish you guys would've settled this out of court because I don't know what to do with you." If I grant the petition's request, I can often modify the relief requested [in an attempt to even out the decision], but still one side has got to win and one side has got to lose. I could cite good precedents on either side, and it's no good worrying about the appeals court because there's no telling what they would do with it should the judge's decision be appealed.

In situations such as this, judges have little choice but to turn to their personal value sets to determine how to resolve the cases. Decision making is affected by local attitudes and traditions or by the judge's perception of the public mood or the will of the current state legislature or administration.

When a Case Concerns New Areas of the Law

Researchers also set aside the legal subculture model and turn to the democratic subculture approach when jurists are asked to resolve new types of policy questions for which statutory law and appellate court guidelines are virtually absent.

In late 2001 the New Jersey Supreme Court was asked to decide a novel question: May a man have the frozen embryos he and his ex-wife created implanted in the body of the man's new wife? The case involved Mr. "M. B." and Mrs. "J. B.," who created seven embryos during the course of their marriage and had them frozen for future use. When the couple divorced in 1998, their divorce settlement left open the question of custody of the embryos. Mr. "M. B." remarried and wished to have the frozen embryos implanted in his new wife, but the first wife objected, stating that she "did not want to become a parent against her will."

The New Jersey Supreme Court ruled that Mr. "M. B." could retain the embryos or have them destroyed, but he could not have them implanted in his new wife. As one Atlanta attorney who has handled several cases involving disputed embryos said of this case: "There is really no guiding principle nationwide in these cases. There are very few states that have looked at the issue." [38]

The Judge's Role Conception

In the discussion of which better explains judicial decision making—the rules of the legal subculture or stimuli from the democratic subculture—one other factor must be considered: how judges conceive of their judicial role. Judicial scholars often talk about three basic decision-making categories regarding whether judges should make law when they decide cases. The lawmakers are those judges who take a broad view of the judicial role. Often referred to as activists or innovators, these jurists contend that they can and must make law in their decisions, because the statutory law and appellate guidelines are often ambiguous or do not cover all situations and because legislative intent is frequently impossible to determine.

At the other end of the continuum are the law interpreters, those judges who take a narrow, traditional view of the judicial function. Sometimes called strict constructionists, they do not believe that judges should substitute judicial wisdom for the rightful power of the elected branches of government to make policy. They tend to eschew making innovative decisions that may depart from the literal meaning of controlling precedents.

Midway between the law interpreters and the lawmakers are judges known as pragmatists or judicial realists. They believe that on occasion they are obliged to make law, but that for most cases a decision can be made by consulting the controlling law or appellate court precedents.

Whether judicial decisions are better explained by the legal model or by the democratic model depends not only on the nature of the cases and the state of the controlling law and precedents but also to some degree on how the individual judges evaluate these factors. In virtually every case that comes before them, judges have to determine how much discretion they have and how they wish to exercise it. This process is necessarily subjective, and activist judges will generally find more discretion in a given fact situation than will their more restrained colleagues.

DECISION MAKING IN COLLEGIAL COURTS

Before an analysis of judicial decision making can be complete, a vital difference between trial courts and appellate courts must be recognized. A trial court renders decisions that are largely the product of a single individual, and appellate courts, as **collegial courts,** make decisions through group interaction.

Cue Theory

As long as appeals courts have jurisdiction over a case, the judges must render a decision on the merits. If the judges view a particular case as presenting a trivial question, they will not spend time agonizing over it, but they are still obliged to provide some sort of formal ruling on the substance of the matter. This situation is not the same in all state high courts, however, because a number of them have a degree of discretion over the cases they must review.[39] The judges decide which issues they want to tackle during a given term and which they believe do not merit much attention.

Cue theory is based on the assumption that judges have neither the time nor the desire to wade through myriad pages in the thousands of petitions presented to them each year. Therefore, they presumably must look for cues in each petition—readily identifiable characteristics that trigger a positive response as they skim through the piles of legal documents. Examples of such cues might be whether the government is one of the parties in the case, the nature of the issues presented in the case, or whether there was a split among the judges on the multi-judge court that reviewed the trial court's decision.

Small-Group Analysis

As applied to the judiciary, most **small-group analysis** is based on the thesis that judges want to influence the judgments of their colleagues and to be on the winning side as often as possible. This school of thought assumes that judges' positions are not written in stone from the start but are susceptible to moderation or even to a 180-degree turn on occasion. More specifically, scholars believe that a good deal of interaction and conflict takes place among judges from the time a case is first discussed to the moment the final decision is rendered some weeks or months later. One researcher has referred to the appellate judges' openness to change as **"fluidity."** [40]The way judges relate to one another affects their behavior on the court. Two characteristics in particular seem to carry weight when judges seek to influence their colleagues: personality and intellect. As one researcher put it after interviewing state supreme court justices in Louisiana, Massachusetts, New Jersey, and Pennsylvania: "Generally the judges believed it is important for court members to moderate their own personal idiosyncrasies in order to maintain as much harmony in the group as possible. Such things as arrogance, pride, sense of superiority, and loss of temper were condemned." [41]

The other personal attribute that is part of small-group dynamics is the knowledge and intellectual capacity of the individual judge. A judge with a superior intellect or wide experience in a particular area of the law has a good deal more clout than a jurist who is seen as an intellectual lightweight.

The techniques or strategies that judges use in their conscious (or even unconscious) efforts to maximize their impact on multi-judge courts can be grouped into three general categories: persuasion on the merits, bargaining, and threat of sanctions. Although the tactics overlap and are inherently interrelated, each has a different focus.

Persuasion on the Merits.

The strategy of persuasion on the merits means that because of their training and values, judges are open to persuasion based on sound legal reasoning bolstered by legal precedents. Unless judges have taken a hard and fast position from the start, most can be swayed by an articulate and well-reasoned argument from a colleague with a differing opinion. Based on interviews with supreme court justices in four states, one scholar stated:

> When differences become evident, members of the court may attempt to persuade other judges to adopt their views by vigorously presenting their position or arguing the merits of their way of analyzing the case. Because of different amounts of influence exerted by the chief justice or by judges who have special status on the court, certain members of the court may be "persuaded" to abandon their own position and adopt the views of others.[42]

Bargaining.

Bargaining may be a strange word to use in talking about the personal interactions of judges on collegial courts. When students first hear the term, they often think of logrolling, the vote-trading technique that legislators sometimes use. Is this what happens with judges, too? No, there is virtually no such evidence. Bargaining does take place, but it is more subtle and does not involve vote swapping.

To understand how the bargaining process works, it is important to realize that usually more is at stake in the outcome of a decision than whether party A or party B wins. Judges also have to discuss such questions as these: How broad should the decision be? Should they suggest in their written opinion that this case is unique, or should they open the gates and encourage other suits of this nature? Should they overturn what appears to be the controlling precedent, or should they "distinguish around" it and let the precedent stand? Should they base their decision on constitutional grounds, or should they allow the victor to win on more technical and restrictive grounds? In other words, most decisions at the appellate level are not zero-sum games in which the winner automatically takes all. Important supplementary issues almost always have to be discussed or bargained for.

Threat of Sanctions.

In addition to persuasion on the merits and bargaining, there is one other tactic that jurists use in their efforts to maximize their impact on multi-member appellate tribunals—the threat of sanctions. Basically, three sanctions against colleagues can be invoked: the vote, the willingness to write a strong dissenting opinion, and the threat to "go public."

For the most part, the potential effect of a threat to dissent from the majority depends on how small that majority is. If the initial vote of a three-judge appellate court was 3–0, one member's threat to dissent would not be all that serious; there would still be a 2–1 majority. Conversely, if a preliminary state supreme court conference vote was 5–4, the threat to defect by one of those five would be of concern to the remaining four.

State judges may sometimes feel the need for unanimity in certain types of cases. One justice on the New Jersey Supreme Court told a researcher: "We did have a case where we felt a unanimous opinion was necessary. No one felt strongly about a dissent, so no dissents were made.... A religious case, for example, needs a unanimous decision. Courts don't try to be divisive on this." [43]

The willingness of a judge to write a strong dissent depends on the circumstances for its effectiveness. Sometimes a dissent may be regarded as no more than a nuisance or the fruit of judicial egomania. On other occasions it may be viewed as likely to weaken the impact of the majority opinion. Also, the effectiveness of this threat differs significantly from state to state because the dissent rate varies highly according to whether the supreme court has discretionary or mandatory jurisdiction.[44]

On rare occasions an appellate judge may use the ultimate weapon against colleagues—public exposure. Such strong medicine is usually meted out only when a jurist believes a colleague (or a group of judges) has violated the basic rules of the game. The judge then threatens to hang out the dirty linen for all to see.

The Special Role of State Supreme Court Chief Justices.

The heads of the multi-judge state supreme courts have a number of special duties and responsibilities that constitute still another ingredient in the recipe for small-group interaction. To some extent, the powers and leadership potential of state chief justices mirror those of the U.S. chief justice, but significant differences exist, not only between the federal and state levels but also from one state to another. At the national level, the chief justice is appointed by the president with the advice and consent of the Senate. In some states—such as Michigan—the chief justice is chosen by fellow associate justices; in Texas and Ohio the chief justices are elected directly by the people.[45]

The states also differ in to whether the chief justice has the most power in the assignment of opinions. Only four states follow closely the practice of the U.S. Supreme Court in assigning opinions. In more than a quarter of the states the chief justice assigns opinions in all cases, whether the chief is in the majority or not.[46] Well over half of the states use an automatic method of opinion assignment, whereby a justice either draws cases by lot or receives them by rotation. In less than half of the twenty states that use the rotation system, the assignments hold only if the justice to whom the case is assigned is in the majority. On these different methods of opinion assignment, one group of researchers has concluded, "A chief justice who is an extraordinary leader can make the court perform more effectively and efficiently by using selective opinion assignment. A court without an extraordinary leader may be better served by a rotational method of assignment." [47]

As with the U.S. chief justice, nothing inherent in the office guarantees that a state supreme court chief justice will be an active and effective leader. Intellect, personality, political skills, and a fair degree of happenstance still interact and blend in mysterious ways to create chief justices whom court watchers term either "great" or "ineffective."

SMALL-GROUP INTERACTION

It is unclear how many final outcomes are determined by small-group dynamics. What is clear is that they are a major factor in the writing of the majority opinion and in setting forth its parameters and corollaries. Because scholars still lack a precise measure of the impact of small-group interaction, some researchers have developed analytic approaches that seek to explain and analyze this phenomenon with greater and more quantifiable precision. The first of these approaches is **attitude theory;** the others are variations of what is called the rational choice model.

Attitude Theory

This approach rests on the assumption that judges–particularly appellate jurists—view cases primarily in terms of the broad political and socioeconomic issues they raise and that they generally respond to these issues in accordance with their personal values and attitudes. The judges' official reasons for their decisions (found in their published opinions) are regarded as mere rationalizations.

Suppose that Judge X strongly believes that the government should never tamper with freedom of the press. If a case comes before the court in which censorship is the central issue, Judge X will follow her convictions and vote on the side of the news media. Her written opinion may be full of impressive legal citations, quotations from eminent law reviews, or lofty discussions of the importance of maximum freedom of expression in a democracy. But all of this, the scholars of attitude theory contend, is only a rationalization after the fact. The real reason for Judge X's vote was her strong dislike for the concept of government censorship.

The attitude theorists do not claim that their decision-making models explain everything, and they do not deny that judges must often decide cases against the grain of their personal values. Nevertheless, supporters of the judicial attitude approach contend that it can explain a significant portion of judicial behavior and is well worth the research time and effort that such studies require.

Rational Choice Theory

The **rational choice theory** by no means rejects the basic assumption of attitude theory. Rational choice theorists generally agree that appellate court jurists are primarily motivated by their personal, deeply felt attitudes about public policy and vote accordingly in their judicial decisions. But the rational choice school contends that there is more to it than that, and that the attitudinal position is somewhat simplistic.

These theorists contend that goal-directed judges operate in what they call "strategic" or "interdependent decision-making contexts." The judges realize that the fate of their policy goals often depends on the values of other decision makers, such as their colleagues on the bench, the governor, and members of the state legislature. The judges must often include in their calculus not only what they personally want as a case outcome but also how such an outcome might be affected by the decisions of these other actors. In other words, they engage in **strategic behavior.**

Rational choice theory, then, is not a rejection of the attitudinal model but argues that attitude theorists are too narrow in their approach. The rational choice school suggests that judges often consider in their decision making the possible responses of other political actors—sometimes even going so far as to invite some of these other actors to modify or supplement the high court's decisions.

SUMMARY

State court judges make millions of decisions each year, and scholars have sought to explain the thinking behind these decisions. Two schools of thought have emerged. One theory is based on the rules and procedures of the legal subculture. Judges' decisions, according to this model are the product of traditional legal reasoning and adherence to precedent and judicial self-restraint. The other school of thought, the realist-behavioralist approach, holds that judges are influenced in their decision making by factors such as political party affiliation, local values and attitudes, public opinion, and pressures from the governor and state legislature. In other words, stimuli from this democratic subculture must also be considered if one is to fully understand decision making by state judges.

In some important ways, decision making by judges on collegial appellate courts is different from decision making by judges acting alone on trial benches. Because of these differences, scholars have devised theories and research techniques to capture the special reality of decision making by state multi-judge appellate courts.

We first focused on the courts' dockets. Just like the U.S. Supreme Court, some state supreme courts have a good deal of discretion to determine which cases they should review. In the context of this discretion, we discussed the importance of cue theory—the attempt by scholars to learn the characteristics of those few cases chosen from the many for supreme court consideration.

We then focused on several separate theoretical approaches to explain the decision making of multi-judge courts: small-group analysis, attitude theory, and the rational choice model. Each of these theoretical models has its own working assumptions and research techniques that are used to glean the explanatory data. Although it is tempting to speculate on which of these several approaches provides the best insights into appellate court behavior, it is probably most fair to say that the jury of judicial scholars is still out.

FURTHER THOUGHT AND DISCUSSION QUESTIONS

1. Should a judge's political party affiliation affect the way he or she makes decisions on the bench? Most Americans would say no, although they prefer to elect their judges and do this on a party basis. Is there an inherent inconsistency in these preferences?

2. Should judges' decisions reflect public opinion? Most Americans would find that offensive, but no less an authority than Chief Justice William H. Rehnquist said it is inevitable and unavoidable that judges reflect public opinion. Sometimes trial judges are encouraged by the appellate courts to reflect the public mood in their decision making.

3. Judges are much more likely in some situations to hand down decisions that reflect their personal values. What are the circumstances that allow one to predict whether a judge will render a decision "in accordance with the law" or in accordance with his or her personal attitudes?

4. When appellate court judges get together to discuss a case and decide its outcome, are their deliberations on a high and lofty plane, or are their motivations and actions no different from those of any group of ordinary citizens acting as an organized committee?

Notes

1. Richard J. Richardson and Kenneth N. Vines, *The Politics of Federal Courts* (Boston: Little, Brown, 1970). Although Richardson and Vines developed their model primarily for federal courts, we believe that their hypotheses and conclusions are equally true for state judges.
2. Edward H. Levi, *An Introduction to Legal Reasoning* (Chicago: University of Chicago Press, 1948), 1–2.
3. *Lane v. Wilson*, 307 U.S. 268 (1939); and *Gomillion v. Lightfoot*, 364 U.S. 339 (1960).
4. *Lane*, 307 U.S. at 275.
5. *Gomillion*, 364 U.S. at 342.
6. Donald J. Farole Jr., "Problem Solving and the American Bench: A National Survey of Trial Court Judges," *Justice System Journal* 30 (2009): 50–69.
7. Henry J. Abraham, *The Judicial Process*, 7th ed. (New York: Oxford University Press, 1998), chap. 9.
8. *Evers v. Jackson Municipal Separate School District*, 232 F. Supp. 241 (1964).
9. Ibid., 247.
10. Ibid., 249.
11. Ibid., 255.
12. Richardson and Vines, *The Politics of Federal Courts*, 8–9.
13. Steven Vago, *Law and Society*, 5th ed. (Englewood Cliffs, N.J.: Prentice Hall, 1997), 354.
14. Steven Vago, *Law and Society*, 6th ed. (Upper Saddle River, N.J.: Prentice Hall, 2000), chap. 9.
15. Oliver Wendell Holmes Jr., *The Common Law* (Boston: Little, Brown, 1881), 1–2.
16. Jerome Frank, *Courts on Trial: Myth and Reality in American Justice* (Princeton, N.J.: Princeton University Press, 1950), 151.
17. Donald Dale Jackson, *Judges* (New York: Atheneum, 1974), 18.
18. One recent study noted that between 1959 and 1998, 140 books, articles, dissertations, and conference papers reported empirical data showing a link between judges' political party affiliation and their judicial behavior. Daniel R. Pinello, "Linking Party to Judicial Ideology in American Courts: A Meta-Analysis," *Justice System Journal* 20 (1999): 219–254.
19. David W. Adamany, "The Party Variable in Judges' Voting: Conceptual Notes and a Case Study," *American Political Science Review* 63 (1969): 59.
20. S. Sidney Ulmer, "The Political Party Variable in the Michigan Supreme Court," *Journal of Public Law* 11 (1962): 352–362; and Malcolm M. Feeley, "Another Look at the 'Party Variable' in Judicial Decision-Making: An Analysis of the Michigan Supreme Court," *Polity* 4 (1971): 91–104.
21. Philip L. Dubois, "The Illusion of Judicial Consensus Revisited: Partisan Conflict on an Intermediate State Court of Appeals," *American Journal of Political Science* 32 (1988): 946–967.

22. Ibid., 953–954.
23. For a good bibliography of the literature on partisan voting patterns among state judges, see ibid., 965–967. Also, see the literature review in Paul R. Brace and Melinda Gann Hall, "Studying Courts Comparatively: The View from the American States," *Political Research Quarterly* 48 (1995): 5–29.
24. Laura Langer and Teena Wilhelm, "The Ideology of State Supreme Court Chief Justices," *Judicature* 89 (2005): 86.
25. This discussion is based on material taken from Martin A. Levin, *Urban Politics and the Criminal Courts* (Chicago: University of Chicago Press, 1977).
26. Ibid., 136–142.
27. Ibid.
28. Ibid., 142–147.
29. Henry R. Glick, *Courts, Politics, and Justice,* 3rd ed. (New York: McGraw-Hill, 1993), 321.
30. For examples of these earlier studies, see Glen T. Broach et al., "State Political Culture and Sentence Severity in Federal District Courts," *Criminology* 16 (1978): 373–382; and Ronald Stidham and Robert A. Carp, "Trial Courts' Responses to Supreme Court Policy Changes: Three Case Studies," *Law and Policy Quarterly* 4 (1982): 215–335.
31. James H. Kuklinski and John E. Stanga, "Political Participation and Government Responsiveness: The Behavior of California Superior Courts," *American Political Science Review* 73 (1979): 1090–9.
32. Melinda Gann Hall, "Electoral Politics and Strategic Voting in State Supreme Courts," *Journal of Politics* 54 (1992): 427.
33. Paul Brace and Brent D. Boyea, "State Public Opinion, the Death Penalty, and the Practice of Electing Judges," *American Journal of Political Science* 52 (2008):
34. "Dallas Judge Apologizes for 'Poor Choice of Words,' " *Montrose Voice,* December 23, 1988, 5.
35. "Overheard," *Newsweek,* January 2, 1989, 13.
36. Clay Robison, "Perry's Prediction on Suit Draws Fire," *Houston Chronicle,* June 9, 2004.
37. G. Alan Tarr and Mary Cornelia Aldis Porter, *State Supreme Courts in State and Nation* (New Haven, Conn.: Yale University Press, 1988), chap. 2.
38. Ibid., 45.
39. Roger D. Groot, "The Effects of an Intermediate Appellate Court on the Supreme Court Product: The North Carolina Experience," *Wake Forest Law Review* 7 (1971): 548–572.
40. Tarr and Porter, *State Supreme Courts in State and Nation,* 51.
41. *Lawrence v. Texas,* 539 U.S. 558 (2003).
42. Keith B. Richburg, "Calif. Ruling Shows Hurdles Remain for Gay Marriage," *Washington Post,* May 27, 2009.
43. E. J. Dionne Jr., "Obama Hopes Sotomayor is the Remedy for Roberts," *Houston Chronicle,* May 28, 2009, B9.
44. John P. McAlpin, "Father Not Allowed to Donate Embryos," *Houston Chronicle,* August 15, 2001.
45. See Tarr and Portis, *State Supreme Courts in State and Nation,* 49.
46. J. Woodford Howard Jr., "On the Fluidity of Judicial Choice," *American Political Science Review* 62 (1968): 43–57.
47. Henry R. Glick, *Supreme Courts in State Politics* (New York: Basic Books, 1971), 59.

SUGGESTED RESOURCES

American Judicature Society Web Site. Available online at www.ajs.org. This nonpartisan organization produces very readable articles on law-related topics and on decision making by state judges.

Burton, Steven J. *An Introduction to Law and Legal Reasoning*, 2nd ed. New York: Aspen Publishers, 1995. Explains what it has traditionally meant to "think like a judge"; explores the judicial reasoning process.

Carter, Lief H., and Thomas F. Burke. *Reason in Law*, 7th ed. New York: Pearson Education, 2004. An excellent discussion of how judges think and reason and a good explication of the legal subculture.

Epstein, Lee, ed. *Contemplating Courts*. Washington, D.C.: CQ Press. 1995. A classic reader in judicial decision making; the contributors are among the best scholars in the field.

Epstein, Lee, and Jack Knight. *The Choices Justices Make*. Washington, D.C.: CQ Press. 1988. An excellent summary of the several theoretical approaches to the study of appellate court decision making.

Justice System Journal 22 (2001). The entire issue is devoted to research on state courts; some of the articles contain data that could be used to perform studies of state appellate judge behavior.

Murphy, Walter F., C. Herman Pritchett, and Lee Epstein. *Courts, Judges, and Politics*, 5th ed., Part Four. New York: McGraw-Hill, 2002. An excellent collection of edited essays on both traditional and modern ways of explaining how judges make decisions.

O'Brien, David. *Judges on Judging: Views from the Bench*. Washington, D.C.: CQ Press. 2008. A collection of essays, mainly by appellate judges, about how such jurists ought to carry out their functions and duties.

Posner, Richard A. *How Judges Think*. Cambridge: Harvard University Press, 2008. A distinguished federal judge and judicial scholar explains the processes and calculations that judges employ in arriving at their judicial decisions.

Richardson, Richard J., and Kenneth N. Vines. *The Politics of Federal Courts: Lower Courts in the United States*. Boston: Little, Brown, 1970. A classic discussion of the influences of both the legal subculture and the democratic subculture on judicial decision making.

Tarr, G. Alan, and Mary Cornelia Aldis Porter. *State Supreme Courts in State and Nation*.

New Haven, Conn.: Yale University Press, 1988. An analysis of decision making at the state supreme court level, with specific focus on three selected state courts.

Robert A. Carp, Ronald Stidham, and Kenneth L. Manning, *The State Courts*, (Washington, DC: CQ Press, 2010).

7. IMPLEMENTATION AND IMPACT OF JUDICIAL POLICIES

In the previous chapter we focused on decision making by judges. In this chapter we extend the discussion to examine what happens after a decision has been reached. Decisions made by judges are not self-executing, and a wide variety of individuals—other judges, public officials, even private citizens—may be called on to implement a court's decisions. In this chapter we look at the various actors involved in the implementation process, their reactions to judicial policies, and the methods they may use to respond to a court's decision.

Depending on the nature of the court's decision, the judicial policy may have a narrow or a broad impact. A suit for damages incurred in an automobile accident would directly affect only the persons involved and perhaps their immediate families. But the famous *Gideon v. Wainwright* decision has directly affected millions of people in one way or another.[1] In *Gideon* the Supreme Court held that states must provide an attorney for indigent defendants in felony trials. Scores of people—defendants, state judges, lawyers, taxpayers—have felt the effects of that judicial policy. As we discuss the implementation process, we also look at the impact of judicial policymaking on society.

THE IMPACT OF HIGHER COURT DECISIONS ON LOWER COURTS

Americans often view the appellate courts as most likely to be involved in policymaking and the trial courts as norm enforcers rather than policymakers. Given this traditional view, the picture that often emerges portrays the appellate court as making a decision that is then implemented by a lower court. In short, some envision a judicial bureaucracy with a hierarchy of courts much like superiors and subordinates.[2] More recent studies have cast doubt on this bureaucracy theory, arguing that "most of the work of the lower courts seems less dependent on the highest court than ... bureaucracy [theory] would indicate." [3] In other words, lower court judges have a great deal of independence from the appellate courts and may be viewed as "independent actors ... who will not follow the lead of higher courts unless conditions are favorable for their doing so." [4] For example, not all trial judges immediately enforced the Supreme Court's public school desegregation decision.[5] Some judges allowed school districts to engage in a variety of tactics ranging from evasion to postponement of the Supreme Court mandate.[6]

Lower Court Discretion

Why do the lower court judges have so much discretion when implementing a higher court's policy? In part, the answer may be found in the structure of the U.S. judicial system. The judiciary has always been characterized by independence, decentralization, and individualism. Federal judges are protected by life tenure and traditionally have been able to run their courts as they see fit. Disciplinary measures are not at all common, and federal judges have historically had little fear of impeachment. To retain their positions, the state trial court judges do not have to worry about the appellate courts in their system. They simply have to keep the electorate satisfied. In short, lower court judges have a good deal of freedom to make their own decisions and respond to upper court rulings in their own way.

The discretion exercised by a lower court judge may also be a product of the higher court's decision itself. Following the famous school desegregation decision in 1954, the Supreme Court heard further arguments on the best way to implement its new policy. In 1955 it handed down its decision in *Brown v. Board of Education of Topeka II.*[7] In that case the Court was faced with two major questions: (1) How soon are the public schools to start desegregating? (2) How much time should they be given to complete the process? Trial judges given the task of enforcing the high court's ruling were told that the public schools should make a prompt and reasonable start and then proceed with all deliberate speed to bring about desegregation. What constitutes a prompt and reasonable start? How rapidly must a school district proceed to be moving with "all deliberate speed"? Because the Supreme Court justices did not provide specific answers to these questions, many lower court judges were faced with school districts that continued to drag their feet while claiming they were acting within the Supreme Court's guidelines.

A second example may be found in two environmental law cases decided on June 19, 2006.[8] Both cases involved defining which wetlands the federal government could regulate under the Clean Water Act of 1972. As the justices were unable to reach a consensus on the proper definition, the Court remanded the cases for further proceedings. In a separate concurring opinion, Chief Justice John G. Roberts Jr. stated:

> It is unfortunate that no opinion commands a majority of the Court on precisely how to read Congress' limits on the reach of the Clean Water Act. Lower courts and regulated entities will now have to feel their way on a case-by-case basis.[9]

Therefore, trial court judges implementing either of the policies described could exercise a high degree of freedom and still legitimately say that they were in compliance with the Supreme Court's mandate. Although not all high court decisions allow such discretion, a good number of them do. Opinions that are ambiguous or poorly written are almost certain to encounter problems during the implementation process.

A court's decision may be unclear for several reasons. Sometimes the issue or subject matter may be so complex that it is difficult to fashion a clear policy. In obscenity cases the Supreme Court has had little difficulty in deciding that pornographic material is not entitled to constitutional protection. Defining obscenity has proved to be another matter. Phrases such as "prurient interest," "patently offensive," "contemporary community standards," and "lacks serious literary, artistic, political, or scientific value" have become commonplace in obscenity opinions. These terms leave considerable room for subjective interpretation. It is little wonder that one Supreme Court justice admitted that he could not define obscenity but added, "I know it when I see it." [10]

Policies established by collegial courts are often ambiguous because the majority opinion is written to accommodate several judges. At times such opinions read more like committee reports than forceful, decisive statements. The majority opinion may also be accompanied by several concurring opinions. When this happens, lower court judges lack a clear-cut precedent to follow. Death penalty cases serve as an example. In 1972 the Supreme Court struck down the death penalty in several states, but for a variety of reasons. Some justices opposed the death penalty per se, on the ground that it constitutes cruel and unusual punishment in violation of the Eighth Amendment to the Constitution. Others voted to strike down the state laws because they were applied in a discriminatory manner.[11] The uncertainty created by the 1972 decision affected not only lower court judges but also state legislatures. The states passed a rash of widely divergent death penalty statutes and caused a considerable amount of new litigation.

A lower court judge's discretion in the implementation process may also be affected by the manner in which a higher court's policy is communicated. The first step in implementing a judicial policy is to learn of the new appellate court ruling. Presumably, lower court judges automatically are made aware of a higher court's decision, but that is not always so. The court from which a case has been appealed will certainly be informed of the decision.

The Virginia Supreme Court was told of the U.S. Supreme Court's decision in *Atkins v. Commonwealth of Virginia* (discussed below) because its earlier decision was reversed, and the case was remanded to it for further action. Systematic formal efforts are not, however, made to inform other courts of the decision or to see that lower court judges have access to a copy of the opinion. The decisions that contain the new judicial policy are simply made available to the public in printed form or on the Internet, and judges are expected to read them if they have the time and inclination.

Opinions of the Supreme Court, lower federal courts, and state appellate courts are available in a large number of courthouse, law school, and university libraries and on the Internet. Some court opinions can now be read on the same day they are handed down or within just a few days, but, this widespread availability does not guarantee that they will be read and clearly understood. One complication is that many lower level state judges, such as justices of the peace and juvenile court judges, are nonlawyers with little interest or skill in reading complex judicial decisions.[12] Finally, even those judges who have an interest in higher court decisions and the ability to understand them do not have adequate time to keep abreast of all the new opinions.

Given these problems, how do judges become aware of upper court decisions? One way is to hear of them from lawyers presenting cases in the lower courts. It is generally assumed that the opposing attorneys will present relevant precedents in their arguments before the judge. Those judges who are fortunate enough to have law clerks may also rely on them to search out recent decisions from higher courts.

Therefore some higher court policies are not quickly and strictly enforced because lower court judges are not aware of them. Even those of which they are aware may not be as clear as a lower court judge might like. Either reason contributes to the discretion exercised by lower court judges placed in the position of having to implement judicial policies.

Interpretation by Lower Courts

One study noted that "important policy announcements almost always require interpretation by someone other than the policymaker." [13] This is certainly true of judicial policies established by appellate courts. The first exercising of a lower court judge's discretion may be to interpret what the higher court's decision means.

Consider an example from the U.S. Supreme Court decision announced on June 20, 2002, in *Atkins v. Commonwealth of Virginia.*[14] In this case the justices addressed the specific question of whether the U.S. Constitution prohibits the imposition of the death penalty on convicted murderers suffering mental retardation or whether such offenders are eligible for executions.[15]

By a 6–3 vote the Court held that the Eighth Amendment bars the execution of mentally retarded individuals. The matter of defining mental retardation, however, was left to Virginia and the other nineteen states that had previously permitted such executions.[16]

At the close of its majority opinion the Court simply declared that "the judgment of the Virginia Supreme Court is reversed and the case is remanded for further proceedings not inconsistent with this opinion." [17] The Virginia Supreme Court responded by ruling on June 6, 2003, that Daryl Atkins's death sentence would not immediately be reduced to life in prison. Instead, it returned the case to the trial court that had initially sentenced Atkins for a hearing on whether he met the state's definition of mental retardation.

After nine days of testimony and thirteen hours of deliberation the jury voted unanimously that Atkins had not proven by a preponderance of the evidence that he was in fact retarded. The trial judge, Prentis Smiley Jr., then set December 2, 2005, as Atkins's execution date.

Atkins's defense team then appealed to the Virginia Supreme Court, citing thirty-eight legal errors made during the retardation hearing.[18] On June 8, 2006, the Virginia Supreme Court unanimously ruled that the trial judge may have improperly influenced the jury's decision by providing too much information about previous decisions of the case. Also, it ruled that a witness called by the state was not qualified under state law to provide an expert conclusion regarding Atkins's mental retardation. The case was sent back to the trial court for a second hearing to determine if Atkins was mentally retarded.

As the prosecution and defense prepared for another hearing on the retardation issue, a surprise occurred. An attorney for William Jones, Atkins's codefendant in the original murder trial, came forward with a claim that the prosecutor's office had engaged in misconduct in its interrogation of Jones, which might have changed the course of Atkins's original trial.[19] The trial judge decided that he had to deal with the misconduct issue before holding another hearing on whether Atkins was mentally retarded.

The issue was resolved when Judge Smiley ruled that misconduct had indeed occurred during the first trial. He then invoked his discretionary power under Virginia law to alter Atkins's sentence. "At precisely 5:00 p.m. on January 16, 2008, Prentis Smiley commuted Atkins's sentence to life in prison...." [20] More than a decade after Atkins's original murder conviction the case was resolved by the Virginia courts.

The manner in which a lower court judge interprets a policy established by a higher court depends on a number of factors. Many policies are not clearly stated. Reasonable people therefore may disagree over the proper interpretation. Even policy pronouncements that do not suffer from ambiguity are sometimes interpreted differently by different judges.

A judge's personal policy preferences will also affect the interpretation he gives to a higher court policy. Judges come to the courts with their own unique background characteristics. Some are Republicans, others are Democrats; one judge may be liberal, another conservative. They come from different regions of the country. Some have been prosecutors; others have been defense or corporate lawyers. A policy enthusiastically embraced by some judges may be totally rejected by others.

Strategies Used by Lower Courts

Appellate court policies are open to different interpretations. Those who favor and accept a higher court's policy will naturally try to enforce it and perhaps even expand on it. Those who dislike a higher court's policy decision may implement it sparingly or only under duress.

A judge who basically disagrees with a policy established by a higher court can use a number of strategies. One rarely used strategy is defiance, whereby a judge simply does not apply the higher court's policy in a case before a lower court. One study of judicial implementation offers this example:

> Desegregation brought out considerable trial court defiance; in one extreme case, a Birmingham, Alabama, municipal judge not only refused to follow Supreme Court decisions desegregating municipal facilities but also declared the Fourteenth Amendment unconstitutional.[21]

Such outright defiance is highly unusual. A study of the libel decisions of the U.S. courts of appeals between 1964 and 1974 did not find a single case of noncompliance with Supreme Court mandates.[22] Another study, focusing on compliance with the Supreme Court's *Miranda v. Arizona*[23] decision, found only one instance of possible noncompliance and twelve decisions that could be classified as narrow compliance among the 250 cases studied.[24]

Another strategy often used by judges not favorably inclined toward a higher court policy is to avoid having to apply the policy. Sometimes a case may be disposed of on technical or procedural grounds so that the judge does not have to rule on the merits of the case. It may be determined, for example, that the plaintiff does not have standing to sue or that the case has become moot because the issue was resolved before the trial began. Lower court judges sometimes avoid accepting a policy by declaring a portion of the higher court decision to be dicta. Dicta refers to the part of the opinion that does not contribute to the central logic of the decision. It may be useful as guidance but it is not seen as binding. What constitutes dicta is open to interpretation.

Yet another often-used strategy is to apply the policy as narrowly as possible. A lower court judge may rule that a precedent is not controlling because of factual differences between the higher court case and the one before the lower courts. Therefore precedent does not have to be followed.

As noted in Chapter 2, state court judges faced with interpreting or implementing policies on civil liberties often rely on what is termed new judicial federalism, an idea that originated in the early 1970s, primarily as a result of Warren E. Burger's appointment as chief justice of the United States. Many civil libertarians, fearful that the new Burger Court would erode or overturn major Warren Court decisions, began to look to state bills of rights as alternative bases for their court claims. The Burger Court encouraged a return to state constitutions by pointing out that the states could offer greater protection under their own bills of rights than was available under the federal Bill of Rights.

Initially, courts used this approach to circumvent specific Burger Court decisions. Since that time, however, "state courts have undertaken major initiatives involving school finance, exclusionary zoning, the rights of defendants, and the right to privacy." [25]

Some studies have cautioned against too much optimism among those who advocate reliance on state constitutions as a way to avoid conservative precedents espoused by the Burger, Rehnquist, and Roberts Courts. In separate examinations of criminal justice decisions from all fifty state high courts, Barry Latzer and Michael Esler concluded that state supreme courts continue to rely on federal law in the vast majority of their decisions.[26]

Not all lower court judges are opposed to a policy announced by a higher court. Some judges have risked social ostracism and various kinds of harassment to implement policies they believed in even though these policies were not popular in their communities.[27]

A judge who is in basic agreement with a higher court policy is likely to give that policy as broad an application as possible. The precedent might be expanded to apply to other areas.

In *Griswold v. Connecticut* (1965) the Supreme Court held that a Connecticut statute forbidding the use of birth control devices was unconstitutional because it infringed on a married couple's constitutional right to privacy.[28] In other words, the Court said the use of birth control devices is a personal decision to be made without interference from the state. Five years later, a three-judge federal district court expanded the *Griswold* precedent to justify its finding that the Texas abortion statute was unconstitutional.[29] The court ruled that the law infringed on an unmarried woman's right of privacy to decide, at least during the first trimester of pregnancy, whether to obtain an abortion. The lower court therefore went further than the Supreme Court in striking down state involvement in such matters.

Influences on Lower Court Judges

Lower courts are not slaves of the higher courts when implementing judicial policies. They have a great degree of independence and discretion. At times the lower courts must decide cases for which the higher courts have not provided precise standards, and the lower court judges must turn elsewhere for guidance in deciding a case before them.

One study notes that in such a position lower court judges "may take their cues on how to decide a particular case from a wide variety of factors including their party affiliation, their ideology, or their regional norms." [30] Several analyses point out that differences between Democratic and Republican lower court judges are especially pronounced when Supreme Court rulings are ambiguous, when there is a transition from one Supreme Court period to another, or when the issue area is so new and controversial that more definite standards have not yet been formulated.[31]

Regional norms have also been mentioned prominently in the literature as having an influence on lower court judges when they interpret and apply higher court decisions.[32] One study found that "federal judges tend to be more vigilant in enforcing national desegregation standards in remote areas than when similar issues arise within the judge's immediate work/residence locale." The prevailing local norms may mean that "when faced with desegregating his own community a judge may be more concerned with public reaction than when dealing with an outlying area." [33]

OTHER IMPLEMENTERS

In addition to lower court judges and various federal officials, many other actors are involved in the interpretation and implementation of judicial policies.[34]

The implementation of judicial policies, whether the product of the U.S. Supreme Court or a state supreme court, is often carried out by state officials. Many of the Supreme Court's criminal due process decisions, such as *Gideon v. Wainwright* and *Miranda v. Arizona,* have been enforced by state court judges and other state officials.[35] For example, state and local police officers implement the *Miranda* requirement that criminal suspects must be advised of their rights. The *Gideon* ruling that an attorney must be provided at state expense for indigent defendants in felony trials has been implemented by public defenders, local bar associations, and individual court-appointed lawyers.

State legislators and executives are also frequently drawn into the implementation process, often as unwilling participants. A judge who determines that a wrong has been committed may use the power to issue an equitable decree as a way of remedying the wrong. The range of remedies available is broad because cases vary in the issues they raise and the types of relief sought. Among the more common options from which a judge may choose are process remedies, performance standards, and specified remedial actions.[36] Process remedies may include advisory committees, citizen participation, educational programs, evaluation committees, dispute resolution procedures, and special masters. The remedies do not specify a particular form of action. Performance standards call for specific remedies—a certain number of housing units or schools or a certain level of staffing in a prison or mental health facility. The specific means of attaining these goals are left to the discretion of the officials named in the suit. Examples of specified remedial actions are school busing, altered school attendance zones, and changes in the size and condition of prison cells or hospital rooms. This type of remedy gives the defendant no flexibility concerning the specific remedy or the means of attaining it.

Implementation of these remedial decrees often devolves, at least partially, to the state legislatures. An order calling for a certain number of prison cells or a certain number of guards in the prison system might require new state expenditures, which the legislature would have to fund. Similarly, an order to construct more modern mental health facilities or provide more modern equipment would mean an increase in state expenditures. Governors would also naturally participate in carrying out these kinds of remedial decrees because they are heavily involved in state budgeting procedures. Also, governors may sign or veto laws. Some even have a line-item veto power, which permits them to veto certain budget items while approving others.

Judges occasionally appoint certain individuals to assist in carrying out the remedial decree. Special masters are usually given some decision-making authority. Court-appointed monitors are also used in some situations, but they do not relieve the judge of decision-making responsibilities. Instead, the monitor is an information gatherer who reports to the judge on the defendant's progress in complying with the remedial decree.

THE IMPACT OF JUDICIAL POLICIES

So far, our focus has been primarily on the implementation of judicial policies by various government officials, which is entirely appropriate because court decisions are often specifically directed at other public policymakers. As one judicial scholar noted, however, “Supreme Court decisions can and do have significant effects on society.” [37]

Some argue that American courts may be too heavily engaged in making decisions that affect society and too involved in policymaking. This is not always the case, but a few of the policies developed by the courts have had significant effects on society as a whole. Notable examples can be found in the areas of racial equality, criminal due process, and abortion. Even though the judiciary plays a greater role in developing the nation's policies than the framers of the Constitution envisioned, one scholar has observed:

> American courts are not all-powerful institutions. They were designed with severe limitations and placed in a political system of divided

> powers. To ask them to produce significant social reforms is to forget their history and ignore their constraints.[38]

Within this complex framework of competing political and social demands and expectations is a policymaking role for the courts. Because the other two branches of government are sometimes not receptive to the demands of certain segments of society, those who are ignored have only one alternative—to turn to the courts. Civil rights organizations made no real headway until they found the Supreme Court to be a supportive forum for their school desegregation efforts. They were then able to use *Brown* and other decisions as a springboard to attack a variety of areas of discrimination. A champion at a high government level may offer hope to individuals and interest groups.

As civil rights groups attained some success in the federal courts, others were encouraged to use litigation as a strategy. As several scholars have found, supporters of women's rights followed a pattern established by minority groups when they began taking their grievances to the courts.[39] What began as a more narrow pursuit for racial equality was broadened to a quest for equality for other disadvantaged groups in society.

Clearly, the courts can announce policy decisions that attract national attention and perhaps emphasize that other policymakers have failed to act. In this way the judiciary may invite the other branches to exercise their policymaking powers. Follow-up decisions indicate the judiciary's determination to pursue a particular policy and help keep alive the invitation for other policymakers to participate in the endeavor.

All things considered, the courts seem best equipped to develop and implement narrow policies that are less controversial in nature. The policy established in the *Gideon* case provides a good example. The decision that indigent defendants in state criminal trials must be provided with an attorney did not elicit any strong protests. Furthermore, it was a policy that primarily required the support of judges and lawyers; action by Congress and the president was not necessary. A policy of equality for all segments of society, however, is so broad and laden with controversy that it must move beyond the judiciary. As it does so, the courts become simply one part, albeit an important part, of the policymaking process.

SUMMARY

We began this chapter by pointing out that judicial decisions are not self-executing. The courts depend on a variety of individuals, both inside and outside the judicial branch, to carry out their rulings.

Lower court judges are prominent in the implementation process. Our discussion of their role in carrying out decisions of higher courts emphasized the discretion they exercise. Factors that account for the flexibility that rests with the lower court judge include the decentralization of the judicial system and the ambiguity of higher court rulings. We also examined the strategies that lower court judges may use in resisting appellate court decisions they dislike.

Some policies call on state officials to take part in the implementation process. State court judges, for example, were the major players in enforcing the Warren Court's decisions on criminal due process. Local law enforcement officials have also been called on to carry out Supreme Court policies.

The final section of the chapter offered some thoughts on the role of courts in bringing about changes in society. It was noted that the judiciary can act as a kind of beacon for traditionally underrepresented groups seeking to achieve their goals.

FURTHER THOUGHT AND DISCUSSION QUESTIONS

1. What arguments can you make for the level of discretion lower court judges should have when implementing decisions of appellate courts? How does this level of individual discretion affect the application of justice in society?

2. Should the judicial branch have the ability to develop and implement public policy, or should that power belong exclusively to the executive and legislative branches? One of our assumptions in this book is that judges routinely engage in policymaking, but what would judicial decisions look like if they were completely divorced from the context of public policy?

3. What are the major strengths and weaknesses of appellate courts in influencing social policies in the United States?

Notes

1. *Gideon v. Wainwright,* 372 U.S. 335 (1963).
2. For a good description of the bureaucratic theory, see Walter F. Murphy, "Chief Justice Taft and the Lower Court Bureaucracy: A Study in Judicial Administration," *Journal of Politics* 24 (1962): 453–476.
3. Richard J. Richardson and Kenneth N. Vines, *The Politics of Federal Courts* (Boston: Little, Brown, 1970), 144.
4. Lawrence Baum, "Implementation of Judicial Decisions: An Organizational Analysis," *American Politics Quarterly* 4 (1976): 91.
5. The desegregation policy was announced in *Brown v. Board of Education of Topeka,* 347 U.S. 483 (1954). For a study of the lower federal courts involved in implementing *Brown,* see Jack W. Peltason, *Fifty-Eight Lonely Men* (New York: Harcourt, Brace and World, 1961).
6. For an excellent account of the school desegregation struggle in Georgia, see Harrell R. Rodgers Jr. and Charles S. Bullock III, *Coercion to Compliance* (Lexington, Mass.: Lexington Books, 1976).
7. *Brown v. Board of Education of Topeka II,* 349 U.S. 294 (1955).
8. See *Rapanos v. United States* and *Carabell v. United States Army Corps of Engineers,* 547 U.S. 715.
9. Ibid.

10. The statement was made by Justice Potter Stewart in *Jacobellis v. Ohio,* 378 U.S. 184 (1964).

11. *Furman v. Georgia,* 408 U.S. 238 (1972). A good account of the various views held by the justices, as well as the behind-the-scenes events leading to the final decision, may be found in Bob Woodward and Scott Armstrong, *The Brethren: Inside the Supreme Court* (New York: Simon and Schuster, 1979), 205–220.

12. For a good discussion of this point with pertinent examples, see Bradley C. Canon and Charles A. Johnson, *Judicial Policies: Implementation and Impact,* 2nd ed. (Washington, D.C.: CQ Press, 1999), 49–50.

13. Ibid., 29.

14. *Atkins v. Commonwealth of Virginia,* 536 U.S. 304 (2002). An excellent study of this case is provided in Thomas G. Walker, *Eligible for Execution: The Story of the Daryl Atkins Case* (Washington, D.C.: CQ Press, 2009). Our discussion of the case is based on material found in this book.

15. Ibid., 1.

16. Ibid., 242.

17. Ibid., 244.

18. Ibid., 258–259.

19. For a complete account of this claim, see ibid., 262–277.

20. Ibid., 277.

21. Canon and Johnson, *Judicial Policies,* 38.

22. See John Gruhl, "The Supreme Court's Impact on the Law of Libel: Compliance by Lower Federal Courts," *Western Political Quarterly* 33 (1980): 517.

23. *Miranda v. Arizona,* 384 U.S. 436 (1966).

24. See Donald R. Songer and Reginald S. Sheehan, "Supreme Court Impact on Compliance and Outcomes: *Miranda* and *New York Times* in the United States Courts of Appeals," *Western Political Quarterly* 43 (1990): 307.

25. See G. Alan Tarr, *Understanding State Constitutions* (Princeton, N.J.: Princeton University Press, 1998), 166.

26. See Barry Latzer, "The Hidden Conservatism of the State Court Revolution," *Judicature* 74 (1991): 190–197; and Michael Esler, "State Supreme Court Commitment to State Law," *Judicature* 78 (1994): 25–32.

27. See Peltason, *Fifty-Eight Lonely Men;* and Richardson and Vines, The Politics of *Federal Courts,* 98–99.

28. *Griswoldv. Connecticut,* 381 U.S. 479 (1965).

29. *Roe v. Wade,* 314 F. Supp. 1217 (1970).

30. Ronald Stidham and Robert A. Carp, "U.S. Trial Court Reactions to Changes in Civil Rights and Civil Liberties Policies," *Southeastern Political Review* 12 (1984): 7.

31. See, for example, Kathleen L. Barber, "Partisan Values in the Lower Courts: Re-apportionment in Ohio and Michigan," *Case Western Reserve Law Review* 20 (1969): 406–407; Robert A. Carp and C. K. Rowland, *Policymaking and Politics in the Federal District Courts* (Knoxville: University of Tennessee Press, 1983), chap. 2; C. K. Rowland and Robert A. Carp, "A Longitudinal Study of Party Effects on Federal District Court Policy Propensities," *American Journal of Political Science* 24 (1980): 301; and Ronald Stidham, Robert A. Carp, and C. K. Rowland, "Women's Rights before the Federal District Courts, 1971–1977," *American Politics Quarterly* 11 (1983): 214.

32. See, for example, Peltason, *Fifty-Eight Lonely Men;* Kenneth N. Vines, "Federal District Judges and Race Relations Cases in the South," *Journal of Politics* 26 (1964): 338–357; Richardson and Vines, *The Politics of Federal Courts,* 93–100; and Michael W. Giles and Thomas G. Walker, "Judicial Policy-Making and Southern School Segregation," *Journal of Politics* 37 (1975): 917–936.

33. Giles and Walker, "Judicial Policy-Making and Southern School Segregation," 931.

34. One study, for example, analyzed judicial implementation and impact from the standpoint of four populations: an interpreting population, an implementing population, a consumer population, and a secondary population. See Bradley C. Canon and Charles A. Johnson, *Judicial Policies: Implementation and Impact,* 2nd ed. (Washington, D.C.: CQ Press, 1999).
35. *Gideon v. Wainwright,* 372 U.S. 335 (1963); *Miranda v. Arizona,* 384 U.S. 436 (1966).
36. Our discussion of the use of such powers is drawn from Phillip J. Cooper, *Hard Judicial Choices* (New York: Oxford University Press, 1988), 12–14, 342, 348–349.
37. Lawrence Baum, *The Supreme Court,* 8th ed. (Washington, D.C.: CQ Press, 2004), 225.
38. See Gerald N. Rosenberg, *The Hollow Hope: Can Courts Bring about Social Change?* (Chicago: University of Chicago Press, 1991), 343.
39. See Richard C. Cortner, "Strategies and Tactics of Litigants in Constitutional Cases," *Journal of Public Law* 17 (1968): 287–307; Jo Freeman, *The Politics of Women's Liberation* (New York: David McKay, 1975); Leslie Friedman Goldstein, "Sex and the Burger Court: Recent Judicial Policy Making toward Women," in *Race, Sex, and Policy Problems,* ed. Marian Lief Palley and Michael B. Preston (Lexington, Mass.: Lexington Books, 1979), 103–113; and Karen O'Connor, *Women's Organizations' Use of the Courts* (Lexington, Mass.: Heath, 1980).

SUGGESTED RESOURCES

Canon, Bradley C., and Charles A. Johnson. *Judicial Policies: Implementation and Impact,* 2nd ed. Washington, D.C.: CQ Press, 1999. A good study of the process and actors involved in carrying out and enforcing judicial decisions.

Cooper, Phillip J. *Hard Judicial Choices.* New York: Oxford University Press, 1988. Focuses on the use of remedial decrees in carrying out judicial decisions.

Rosenberg, Gerald N. *Hollow Hope: Can Courts Bring about Social Change?* Chicago: University of Chicago Press, 1991. The book focuses on the ability of courts to effect social change.

Walker, Thomas G. *Eligible for Execution: The Story of the Daryl Atkins Case.* Washington,

D.C.: CQ Press, 2009. An excellent study of the case that led to the U.S. Supreme Court's decision that execution of mentally retarded defendants is impermissible under the U.S. Constitution.

Robert A. Carp, Ronald Stidham, and Kenneth L. Manning, *The State Courts*, (Washington, DC: CQ Press, 2010).

8. GLOSSARY

Activism (judicial). The willingness of a judge to inject into a case his or her own personal values about what is good and bad public policy.

Advisory opinions. Rendering a decision on an abstract or hypothetical question (something that American courts are not supposed to do).

Alternative dispute resolution (ADR). Methods of resolving disputes (often with the help of neutral third parties) without a trial. Mediation and arbitration are two well-known ADR techniques.

Amicus curiae ("friend of the court"). A person (or group), not a party to a case, who submits views (usually in the form of written briefs) about how the case should be decided.

Attitude theory. The theory of appellate judge behavior that holds that once the researcher learns the judges' basic set of attitudes, he or she can explain and predict how those judges will vote in the cases that come before them.

Bail. A sum of money put up with the court by the defendant to ensure that he or she will appear at the time of trial.

Bill of information. A statement of the charges against the accused prepared by the prosecutor, which, if approved by a judge, will require the accused to stand trial for the alleged crimes. This device is used in states that do not employ a grand jury.

Civil law. The law that pertains to the relationship between one private citizen and another, and between a private citizen and a corporation, or between one corporation and another.

Class action. A suit brought by persons having similar grievances against a common entity—for example, a group of smokers with lung cancer suing a tobacco company.

Collegial courts. Courts having more than one judge, which are almost always appellate courts.

Common law. A system of law inherited from England based on legal precedents or traditions instead of statutory law or systematic legal codes.

Complaint. A written statement filed by the plaintiff who initiates a civil case. It states the wrongs allegedly committed by the defendant and requests relief from the court.

Concurrent jurisdiction. A situation in which two courts have a legal right to hear the same case.

Conservative. For judges this means support for the prosecution in criminal cases, support for the government in its attempts to restrict freedom of expression, and support for the individual (or corporation) that is being regulated by the government.

Corpus juris. The entire body of law for a particular legal entity.

Court of appeals. A court that is higher than an ordinary trial court and has the function of reviewing or correcting the decisions of trial judges.

Courtroom work group. The regular participants in the day-to-day activities of a particular courtroom. The most visible members of this group are judges, prosecutors, and defense attorneys.

Crime. An offense against the state, punishable by fine, imprisonment, or death.

Criminal law. The law that pertains to offenses against the state itself, actions that may be directed against a person but that are deemed to be offensive to society as a whole—for example, armed robbery or rape.

Cue theory. The theory that Supreme Court justices do not have the time to carefully review all cases that are appealed to them, so they develop shorthand methods of seeking out easy-to-find cues to help them determine whether they want to review a particular case.

Declaratory judgment. When a court outlines the rights of the parties under a statute, a will, or a contract.

En banc ("in the bench" or "as a full bench"). Court sessions with the entire membership of a court participating, not just a smaller panel of judges.

Equity. The realm of the law in which the judge is able to issue a remedy that will either prevent or cure the wrong that is about to happen—for example, an injunction against an illegal strike by a union.

Felony. Any offense for which the penalty may be death or imprisonment in a penitentiary.

Fluidity. The degree that appellate court judges change their opinions between the time a conference vote is taken and the vote is announced in open court.

Grand jury. A body of sixteen to twenty-three citizens who listen to evidence of criminal allegations, which is presented by the prosecutors, and determine whether probable cause exists to believe an individual committed an offense. See also *indictment.*

Impeachment. A method by which a judge may be removed from office. The House of Representatives brings the charge(s), and the Senate, following a trial, convicts by a two-thirds vote of the membership.

Indictment. The decision of a grand jury to order a defendant to stand trial because the jury believes that probable cause exists to warrant a trial.

Judicial realist. One who believes that judges, like other human beings, are influenced by the values and attitudes learned in childhood.

Jurisdiction. The authority of a court to hear and decide legal disputes and to enforce its rulings.

Justiciability. Whether a judge ought to hear or refrain from hearing certain types of cases. It differs from jurisdiction, which pertains to the technical right of a judge to hear a case. For example, lawsuits dealing with political questions are considered nonjusticiable.

Law. A social norm that is sanctioned in threat or in fact by the application of physical force. The party that exercises such physical force, such as a police officer, is recognized by society as legitimately having this kind of authority.

Liberal. For judges this means support for the defendant in criminal cases, support for a broadening position for freedom of expression, and support for the government in its attempt to economically regulate individuals and corporations.

Magistrate. A lower-level judicial official to whom the accused is brought after the arrest. A magistrate has the obligation to inform the accused of the charges against him and to explain his legal rights.

Merit selection. A method of selecting state judges that requires the governor to make the appointment from a short list of names submitted by a special commission established for that purpose. After serving for a brief period of time, the judge must run in a retention election. Voters determine whether the judge should be retained for a full term.

Moot. Describes a case when the basic facts or the status or the parties have significantly changed as the case progresses.

Oral argument. An opportunity for lawyers to summarize their position before the court and to answer the judges' questions.

Ordinance-making power. The power of state governors to fill in the details of legislation of passed by state legislatures.

Original jurisdiction. The court that by law must be the first to hear a particular type of case.

Per curiam ("by the court"). An unsigned opinion of the court, often brief.

Petit jury (or trial jury). A group of citizens who hear the evidence presented by both sides at trial and determine the facts in dispute.

Plea bargain. A bargain or deal that has been struck between the prosecutor and the defendant's attorney whereby some form of leniency is promised in exchange for a guilty plea.

Political question. When the courts refuse to rule because they believe that under the constitution the founders meant that the matter at hand should be dealt with by the legislative or executive branch, the courts are refusing to rule on a political question.

Private law. Deals with the rights and obligations that private individuals and institutions have when they relate to one another.

Pro bono publico ("for the public good"). Usually refers to legal representation undertaken without fee for some charitable or public purpose.

Public law. The relationships that individuals have with the state as a sovereign entity—for example, the tax code, criminal laws, and Social Security legislation.

Rational choice theory. The theory that appellate judges' votes may be explained by knowing more than just their basic attitudes. Judges realize that the fate of their policy goals often depends on the values of other decision makers, such as their colleagues on the bench, the president, and members of Congress.

Role (judicial). How judges view themselves as jurists and the degree to which they believe in judicial activism or judicial self-restraint.

Self-restraint (judicial). The reluctance of a judge to inject into a case his or her own personal ideas of what is good or bad public policy.

Small-group analysis. The theory that appellate court behavior may be explained in part by what social scientists know generally about the decision-making process of small groups of any kind.

Standing. The status of someone who wishes to bring a lawsuit. To have standing the person must have suffered (or be immediately about to suffer) a direct and significant injury.

Stare decisis, doctrine of. ("Stand by what has been decided.") In effect, the tradition of honoring and following previous decisions of the courts and established points of law.

Statutory law. The type of law enacted by a legislative body, such as a state legislature, or a city council.

Strategic behavior. Judges engage in this behavior when they make decisions based upon a consideration of the actions of other judicial and political decision makers.

Trial de novo. A new trial in which the entire case is retried as if no prior trial had occurred.